WRITING HISTORICAL FICTION

WRITING HISTORICAL FICTION

Rhona Martin

St. Martin's Press
New York

WRITING HISTORICAL FICTION. Copyright © 1988 by Rhona Martin.
All rights reserved. Printed in the United States of America. No
part of this book may be used or reproduced in any manner
whatsoever without written permission except in the case of
brief quotations embodied in critical articles or reviews. For
information, address St. Martin's Press, 175 Fifth Avenue,
New York, N.Y. 10010.

Library of Congress Cataloging-in-Publication Data

Martin, Rhona.
          Writing historical fiction / by Rhona Martin.
          p.   cm.
      ISBN 0-312-01848-7
      1. Historical fiction—Authorship.   I. Title.
PN3377.5.H57M37 1988
808.3'81—dc19   87-36689
                                                                CIP

First published in Great Britain by A&C Black (Publishers) Ltd.

First U.S. Edition

10 9 8 7 6 5 4 3 2 1

Contents

1
Why a
Historical?

There are many aspects of writing historical fiction, many problems and many challenges. Some of these are common to all types of writing, others are particular to the genre. A historical can be every bit as gripping a read as a contemporary novel, and may be even more so. An outstanding one will linger in the minds of its readers for many years: Margaret Mitchell's *Gone With the Wind,* one of many notable first novels, is a classic example. But, far from being easier to write than contemporary fiction, it must be faced that historicals are, arguably, more demanding. So let us first have a look at some of the reasons which tempt us to have a go.

Not because it looks easier — it isn't

A historical novel may look like an easy option. This may be your first attempt at writing a book; you want the result to be good, a real page-turner, to be enthusiastically accepted by a publisher. You want to be able to stroll down the main street pretending not to have noticed the eyecatching displays of your novel in its swashbuckling jacket in the window of your local bookshop. You want newspapers and radio stations to ring you up, pleading for interviews, friends to complain that it kept them awake all night because they couldn't put it down. Of course you do — don't we all? So surely, with all that picturesque background imbued with the romance of bygone days, the colourful way of life and the exciting adventures people seemed to have, with all that going for it, won't the author find the job half done, or at any rate made a great deal easier? Well, hold on a minute.

It may well be true that good story-telling is enhanced by the richness of the setting, but don't be deceived: it won't make it any easier. Researching the picturesque background alone can take as much time as the writing if it is to have the ring of truth. The spectacular lives of the great and the famous were by no means mirrored in those of the majority of people struggling along at ground level; for them at least, the 'romance of bygone days' is largely a myth, though their lives are no less interesting for that. It can't have been much fun toiling up and down those romantic spiral stairs to take milord his late night posset, or washing milady's menstrual linen with the aid of cold water and a couple of heavy stones. Both royalty and nobility lived in constant domestic discomfort, and a broken bone or a heavy cold was a genuine hazard to life. Just imagine how the early monarchs would have been dazzled by the creature comforts we all take for granted now. Small wonder that in mediaeval times even their life expectancy was little more than thirty-five years. They had their own ways of making life enjoyable – one of which was to stretch out Christmas to cover twelve whole days, and even Jack and Joan in their one-roomed cottage had their high days and holidays to sweeten the pill.

It is here, in the bringing to life of people as they really were in far-off times, that the fascination of the historical lies, not in the unreal adventures of imagined heroes. You are saying to the reader 'come with me, I want to show you something'. And in doing so, you too will be putting on your main character like a suit of clothes, and entering the past on a voyage of discovery. Like anything worth doing, it offers a challenge which at first glance may be daunting. But the rewards are great, and well worth working for.

Not because 'everybody's doing it'

Beware of being beguiled by a passing trend. The operative word here is 'passing' and it cannot be stressed too strongly. Perhaps you have already written, perhaps published, one or more books, plays or short stories. You keep meeting people who tell you that there is a big boom – or a big slump – in 'hot historicals', romances, family sagas, this or that.

It may be true; but unless you are a very rapid and experienced writer the trend is likely to have passed by the time you have your masterpiece written, submitted (perhaps to several publishing houses before it finds a home), accepted, printed and out on the bookstalls, which may take as much as two to three years. You will be wise to resist the temptation to jump on the wagon.

Much has been said – and written – about the value of market research, of knowing what is in demand and aiming your efforts in the most profitable direction. Find out, you will hear, which publisher handles what you want to write.

So far, so good. But beware of modelling your work too closely on another successful writer, whom we will call 'the great X', even if you are honestly convinced that yours is better. If you suspect that you already have, and are about to offer it to 'X's own publisher, think again. They already have that author on their 'list', and are unlikely to want someone else writing similar books, without the undoubted sales back-up of a famous name. You will be wasting your time in knocking on that door. The doorstep you should be standing on is that of the publisher who hasn't got the great 'X', but wishes he had. If your work is really as good as you hope, he is much more likely to be interested.

Not because it won't need as much storyline – it does

One of the deeper pitfalls lies in imagining that a historical won't need such a strong story as other mainstream fiction. A historical needs a storyline strong enough to hold its own, given the competition for a reader's attention offered by the way of life, habits, beliefs and misconceptions of an earlier period, otherwise the story will be swamped and the action will sag. Leaning too heavily on the background will produce a book which is merely a guided tour of the period. Remember the words of Oliver Goldsmith: 'A book may be amusing with numerous errors, or it may be very dull without a single absurdity.'

This is not to say that sound research is a waste of time. But never forget that a good historical must first be a good novel.

The best reason for writing a historical

There is really only one valid reason for setting a story outside the present day and this is that the situation springs from the period, and could not possibly have happened at any other time. Otherwise you will find yourself with a contemporary story in fancy dress, lacking in depth and not very interesting. You will have wasted all the time you have spent on the research, and might just as well have set it in the present day.

To carry conviction, your characters and the situation in which they find themselves must be of the era in which they live. They must think, act, live and breathe in the way appropriate to their time. This is not to say they will indulge in 'gadzookery', by which I mean language more picturesque than intelligible, but they must not be anachronistic in their outlook or their response to the conflicts and dilemmas of their day. Dramatist John Arden, who wrote *The Roses of Eyam*, a very moving play about the heroism of a tiny village in Derbyshire at the time of the Great Plague of London, says 'A good historical is a scene or a situation from history, focused through individuals.' If we are to succeed, we must never lose sight of this fact.

If you truly want to write that one special story that's been burning a hole in you, and you can satisfy yourself on this count, go ahead. You are on the right lines from the beginning. Don't be put off by anyone, especially not by self-styled experts. Your passion for your theme will carry you through, and it won't matter a damn what gloom anyone else may cast upon your project. This happened to me when I was writing my first novel, *Gallows Wedding*, which dealt with a young girl rendered so desperate by poverty and homelessness after the dissolution of the monasteries that she was ready to marry a criminal off the gallows for the sake of his dubious protection. I was told by experienced writers that it would never find a publisher 'because it would not fit into a category': it was too bloody, too earthy, too violent and all the rest, quite apart from being too historical for a romance and too romantic for a historical. I was wasting my time in writing the wrong book. Chastened, I finished it in secret because it wouldn't leave me alone, and when at last it was timidly submitted in the expectation of rejection, I was amazed to find it not only accepted, but awarded the 'Historical Novel Prize in Memory of Georgette Heyer'. The judges, two of whom were publishers, were looking, among other things, for originality. So if you want to write something really unusual, take heart; it could happen to you, too.

Every writer needs a little streak of pure bloodymindedness, and none more than the writer of historicals. Not too much, so that it becomes impossible to climb down from a too high horse, but just enough to see discouragement as a challenge, to be able to say 'I don't care if no one else wants it, I do and I'm going to finish it.'

It is notoriously difficult to judge the standard of your own work; the one sad thing about teaching is that the students with the most talent are so often those with the least confidence, the most likely to give up in despair.

Don't do it. Perseverance is the name of the game.

2
Thinking Time

In China there was once a maker of tapestries whose works were so striking, so beautiful that they were the envy of all who saw them.

He was an old man, with many students, and inevitably he was asked, 'Tell us the secret of your success.'

'I have no secret,' said the tapestry maker. 'I use the same silks as you do, and the stitches are those I have taught you. The difference is that I have found the golden needle.'

For the Chinese to describe something as golden is to say that it is special, of the greatest possible value. What the old man meant by the golden needle was, of course, his own creativity, something which cannot be taught or acquired, but must be found within oneself.

In writing, as in any other art form, talent is not always immediately apparent; you may have been writing for quite a while before discovering exactly where yours lies. The only way to find out is by trying: don't expect to start out with it so clearly defined that it wins instant recognition. Above all, don't be discouraged if your early efforts go unregarded; it has been said that more talent lies buried than has ever come to light, and confidence and perseverance may eventually win the day.

What you really need to start out with is imagination, combined with creativity. These also are unique to you, and no one can find them for you. Others can teach you the techniques, and this we will try to do; but the itch for storytelling, the imaginative vision that makes you want to step into an unknown situation, to undergo it yourself and involve us in the experience, the indefinable element that takes everything that happens around you and spins it into words in the back of your mind, is something only you can provide. Unless you really *want* to write, enjoy the process and are excited by the thought of it, you may well be happier reading historicals than trying to create them.

If that motivation is truly absent no one else can supply it, for it is a part of you; but that you have it in some measure, or at least are on the verge of it, is suggested by the fact that you have chosen to read this far.

And if talent is there, albeit tucked away and as yet unrecognised, somewhere along the way you will find yourself holding the golden needle in your hand.

So let's to the practicalities. As we have seen, a good historical must first be a good read, and whatever the period of the piece, certain principles hold good. One of the most important is:

The story first and always

Edward Blishen has said 'Writing a novel is like building a house with your nose jammed up against the brickwork, longing to be able to stand back and see the whole thing.'

This is never more true than when writing a historical: there seems to be so much to remember, such a load of information to be held in the mind that the brain begins to ache, when all you can see is the little bit you are working on. And that is only the background! What happens when the story starts to move and gather impetus, more and more characters become involved and the unalterable facts of history start sticking their spokes into your carefully thought-out plot?

Your greatest safeguard here is in sufficient thinking or 'brewing' time before you start. Don't let your enthusiasm tempt you to rush into it; if you do, you will run into difficulties very early on. You must know your characters thoroughly, and have a sound understanding of the times in which they lived, the problems they are faced with and the resolution towards which they will be moving.

You will notice that I have placed little stress on plotting. First let us be clear about what we mean by theme, plot and structure.

Theme

The first thing to remember is that theme is not the same as plot, although the two are often confused. The theme is the basic idea, the concept, if you like, from which your story springs; the point you are making. In simpler terms, what the whole story is about. It will usually be something abstract, such as jealousy, ambition, rebellion against injustice, vengeance, love, obsession, the futility of war, the self-fulfilling prophecy, the agonies of divided loyalty, self-sacrifice, idealism or martyrdom.

The theme is likely to be timeless, while the actual plot, i.e. the scenes and moves through which it is played out, must be firmly keyed to the period. Superstition and prejudice are timeless themes; whether they are shown in the persecution of witches or in present-day racial riots will determine whether the fiction is classifiable as historical or contemporary.

These examples are few and of necessity very simplistic, but there are many ways in which they can be developed.

The theme of war, for example, may be treated very differently – the struggle for a throne, a ruthless duel in the Industrial Revolution, a battle between two individuals – or two doctrines – for dominance of a third, or even the slow destruction of a personality through conflict between incompatible desires.

Martyrdom may be the attribute of a saint; yet self-inflicted, it can equally well be the tiresome characteristic of the victim of a persecution complex.

Ambition which started out laudably enough may become corrupted into avarice, ruthlessness and worse ... the variations are endless. Be sure to give plenty of thought to your theme before reaching your decision. When you have, remember that everything that happens in the course of the story, every word you write, should illustrate it. This is not to say that you should preach – Heaven forfend! The business of the writer is not to express an opinion, but to present the facts and their effect on the characters, and leave the formation of judgement to the reader.

If there are no new themes where is the hope of originality, that elusive quality for which publishers are always looking? It lies in originality of treatment, in looking at a cliché situation and asking yourself 'But what would have *really* happened? How would they really have felt – what would I do/feel/think if it were happening to me? Would I really leap up brandishing a sword? Cry "Unhand me, villain!" and swoon away? Fearlessly scale the castle walls, perhaps to find the windows locked and barred? Or would I try negotiation/kick him where it would do the most good/fall and break my neck or have more good sense than to attempt the climb?' And, bearing in mind the words of Richard Boston, 'Excellence in art comes from making a huge, brave, individual effort to tell the truth,' the choice is yours.

Think about it.

Title

It may seem surprising, but this is where your title becomes important. Thinking about it *before* you start to write will help you enormously. A good title, one which truly represents the book, play or story, is likely to be a distillation of the theme, and will be of great value in keeping you on the right lines as the work progresses. One of the reasons for the dreaded 'writer's block' comes from losing sight of your theme about half-way through. It always makes me uneasy when someone reading a story at a workshop says, 'I haven't thought of a title yet.' All too often, it turns out that the writer hasn't thought about the theme either, with the consequence that quite soon he or she complains of being 'stuck' with that particular story, having run out of anything further to say.

Plot

The plot, except of course to the writer of detection, crime novels or thrillers, is less important than it appears. It is the route map of how a story progresses from the beginning to the end, not its essence. This may sound like heresy, but it is true.

If you have chosen the right characters through which to tell your story, and have set them down in the right situation, they will largely take care of the plot. As a new writer you may be alarmed if your characters seem to 'take over', but rejoice! Your characters are alive and breathing, doing their own thing and making the story happen as they should. Characters who are too easily manipulable tend to be puppets – 'cardboard' as editors and reviewers label them – and will not grip your readers or engage their sympathy. Treat them as suspect. They will be nothing but a liability.

To take an example: you have perhaps decided to tell of a girl placed by her parents in a convent. If she is docile, dedicated and with a strong sense of vocation, you will have a story lacking in drama, since the conflict is likely to be minimal. If, however, she is a strong character with a rebellious spirit, who has perhaps been committed against her inclination, as was often the case at certain periods in history (she may have refused to marry the man selected for her, or have nipped out and made her own arrangements with resultant loss of 'honour' and marriageability), then you have only to stand back and watch the sparks fly! The docile girl, on the other hand, will become more interesting if, having thought she was suited to the religious life, she discovers too late that she is not. In either case, the interest of the story will hinge, not on what you may have decided about her fate, but on what she brings upon herself.

At this point it is interesting to note that convents or 'nunneries' have not always been held in the high esteem they are today, and that in particular periods of history, notably in the time running up to the dissolution by Henry VIII, this contempt was not unwarranted, as the inmates got up to some high old capers and by no means all of their habits were religious. By the time Shakespeare had Hamlet telling Ophelia to hie her to a nunnery, the word had become a slang expression for a brothel! However, we digress.

Never forget that people make history, not the other way about. It then becomes clear that the right characters in the given situation are absolutely essential. If you have achieved this at the outset, you will have few problems with the plot.

Construction

Constructing the novel is undoubtedly one of the most difficult aspects of writing, where many otherwise promising writers lose their way. It is that indefinable something which works invisibly behind the scenes to ensure that the story, whether a novel, a play or a short story (arguably the most difficult form of historical fiction) has shape: a beginning which engages the reader's curiosity, a middle which keeps the pages turning, and an end that combines impact with inevitability and, whether happy or poignant, rounds it off in a way that satisfies. Good construction will ensure that there are no loose ends straggling off into the distance unresolved; no 'one spit and a cough' characters waiting in the wings to say one line, after a detailed introduction suggesting that they are of some significance, and never being seen again; that each chapter break comes at a point where something is about to happen, so that it becomes imperative to start reading the next one, yet without the story swinging dizzily up and down like a roller coaster; that interest is sustained throughout and the action never drags or is clogged by surplus information which the writer finds intriguing but the reader doesn't want to know. And all without anyone noticing it at work. ....

Think of your story as having a shape, within which it is contained as a stage is by the proscenium arch. Personally I always know the main characters, perhaps two or three of them, the opening and the ending; in between I let them have their heads and enjoy the journey with them; as long as the theme is clear and you know where they are heading, it is only necessary to give them an occasional nudge in the right direction.

Don't be too worried about writing in chronological order in the early stages, certainly not with the first draft. It is perfectly permissible, and can be helpful, to write scenes or fragments of dialogue as they come to you, never mind if they belong to a later part of the story. Put them on a clip in roughly the order in which you envisage using them, and work them in when you reach that stage of the work. By doing this you will find that they retain the sparkle that prompted you to write them out of sequence, and will bring new freshness to the writing. You may, of course, find that when you reach that stage of the narrative something much better has evolved, or the story has taken a different turn, in which case nothing is lost: every word you write, whether or not you are able to use it, will have developed the characters and enhanced your understanding of them.

A conscientious craftsman will write and rewrite over several drafts, and this is where you can correct and improve your structure if need be. To some extent it is a matter of instinct, of intuition if you like, to sense whether the construction is sound or not. With time and practice you will reach a stage where you have only to read it through to know.

Much of what has been said so far applies most closely to the novel. It may be that your inclination is toward drama, or to that most difficult of historical forms, the short story.

The short story

The shorter the story, the more expert you need to be in giving a strong flavour of the period, its thinking and conventions, at the same time keeping the action flowing and bringing it to a satisfactory close. These problems are present to some extent in the contemporary 'short', but never as crucially as in the historical. The main problem lies in the setting of the scene. To illustrate: if you say, 'They walked down the street as they talked,' and the time is the present day, the reader has an instant mental picture. Even if the setting is exotic, now that we have the mixed blessing of television you have only to mention the name of the country and most readers will have a fair idea of how it looks. But in a historical there is no such instant recognition; you will have to draw the picture yourself by means of description.

The trick here is to use a few key words to suggest the period. A phrase such as 'under the oversail of the houses' will immediately call up a picture of timbered dwellings of the Tudor period with their projecting upper stories; if the street is cobbled instead of packed earth and slush, the period is likely to be a little later, in say the 17th or 18th centuries, when the increase in horse-drawn traffic had made better roads imperative, at least in towns. A modicum of horse lore and management, by the way, are indispensable to the historical writer; you need a nodding acquaintance at least of the speeds, needs and endurance of the animal, if only to ensure that you do not have your hero or heroine galloping off into the distance on a prancing stallion (most impractical and unmanageable as a steed, by the way) and arriving three hundred miles away the next day on the same horse, miraculously surviving and still fresh!

The dramatist will encounter problems of his own, but unless he is writing for radio will have the advantage of costume to help set the period. It will, however, be essential to have a sound knowledge of costume if only to be able to check that the finished play is not 'dressed' in the fashion of a different age – a problem, incidentally, which is shared with the novelist who finds that his Stuart novel has been jacketed in mediaeval dress!

Sometimes you will hear someone say, 'Oh, I'd love to write a historical, but I couldn't. I'm not a historian.'

Now, this is sad. It means either that the writer really thinks that everyone who writes a historical has a degree in history – very flattering to those who write them but manifestly untrue – or that he feels unable to face the mountain of work that would be needed to attain that standard.

Both of these premises are false. Certainly, you need to have an interest in history, why else would you want to write about it? But it is not necessary to know everything about every period. What you do need is sufficient interest to research your given period thoroughly, and by that I mean not merely the dates of great events but the effect those events had on people at all levels. You will want to know all kinds of details about everyday life, how people ate their food (with or without cutlery), what foods were available and how they cooked and served them, how their homes were furnished at the various levels of society, what they wore, what their diseases were and how they tried to deal with them. You will have to be sure even of which flowers grew in gardens at any specific date, which animals were indigenous, which were imported and when. Did you know, for instance, that at one time monkeys were more popular than lap dogs as pets for the ladies of the well-to-do? The unfortunate cat came nowhere on the scale until relatively recently in history, being mistrusted and persecuted, along with the hare and the billy-goat, as an ally of the devil.

It is neither necessary nor desirable to put in all this information, but you must have it, for it is fatally easy to make a mistake, and if you do, the reader who catches you out will lose trust in you and not believe another word you say. One writer scuttled a perfectly good story by putting lace curtains at the window of a cottage in the reign of Henry VIII, a time when only the rich had as much as a pane of glass, the majority managing with shutters or oiled paper to keep out the weather.

Sound research is the foundation of any good historical. If you are to keep that 'willing suspension of disbelief' so necessary in the reader, you must be sure of your facts. What you are telling us is a fabrication from beginning to end; it is up to you to make it convincing.

This is where research comes to the rescue.

3
Research

At what point should you embark on your research? Should you read it all up first, and then divert your attention to other aspects such as characterisation, dialogue and the rest? Should you look up everything as you go along, or perhaps work out the story first and worry about it afterwards?

There is no one point at which to say, this is where the research comes in; the simple truth is that it comes in first, last and in the middle. First, because without a feeling for the period, a sort of road map by which to travel, you will not get further than page one before you have to go running to the library. And it may well be during your preliminary reading that you chance upon the very incident to fire you with the compulsion to write about it. In the middle, because however thorough you have been, there will always be some small detail you need to know that has escaped your net on the first time around. And lastly, at the end; because that is where you will be going through it to take away the scaffolding, the dates which you have placed as markers for your own reference but which blunt the pace and pleasure for your reader, and also those oddments of extraneous information which so delighted you when you found them but which have no real place in your story.

We have already seen the vital role of research in writing a historical. The next most important thing is to know how much of it to put in and, equally important, how much to leave out. And that, surprisingly enough, is a great deal more than you leave in.

What then, you may ask, is the point of all that studying, if it is not going into the book?

The answer is that if you haven't done it, if you don't have all that back-up information at your fingertips, what you do put in is likely to be wrong. There will be some little detail that escapes your attention and trips you up, and if you don't know it is wrong you can bet your boots that there is some reader, somewhere, who does! And we've seen the likely consequences of that in the previous chapter.

Research, as I've been saying for years, is like an iceberg. Only the tip must show, but the rest of it, the great bulk that lurks invisibly under water, has to be there to support it. If it isn't, the whole thing sinks and your effort will be wasted. But won't the surplus research be wasted? No. Research is never really surplus. There is always another book, in which the very thing you discarded as irrelevant to this one may yet play a major part. How do you decide what is or is not relevant? By asking yourself if it carries the story further; if it doesn't, it is better left out.

But what about all those intriguing titbits you found along the way, surely your readers would be equally fascinated? Not necessarily. We may be itching to know what's happened to A., or how B. is going to resolve her dilemma; if you hold up the action to tell us how the clock worked or the recipe for black bread, we will not love you for it.

If, however, your male character (let's not call him the hero) is a maker of clocks working on a brilliant new idea, or the young girl has to learn how to bake in order to get work she sorely needs, the situation becomes entirely different and the knowledge will be relevant. Even so, it must come at a point in the story where we as readers want to know, not merely be dropped in somewhere inappropriate.

This does not mean that it is not worthwhile to research what might be described as 'trivia', often more intriguing to the reader than dates and politics; precisely the sort of thing that can trip you up is not knowing how long it would have taken to travel from point A to point B by stage-coach, on horseback, in a private retinue or on foot. If you don't know these things – and others like the current state of the roads, of which many were impassable in winter – you can fall into errors so glaring that even the reader who knows nothing about it will sense instantly that there is something not quite right. The ring of truth will be missing and inevitably doubt will set in.

The kind of information you will need in writing fiction is not quite the same as that for writing a biography or a textbook. You will be more concerned with social history than political, although undoubtedly the latter had profound effects on those who had no hand in making it, just as it does today. What you will want to be familiar with are facts such as what kind of fabrics were used in making clothes, what colours were available to the man in the street – not crimson or purple, which dyes were extremely expensive to make, the main reason for their being the traditional colours of royalty – how people washed, if at all, and what conditioned their thinking.

In mediaeval times, for example, the Church of Rome exerted enormous power. Kings could be brought to their knees – and were – by the threat of excommunication. The royal penance for the murder of Thomas à Becket was by no means extravagant for its time.

Likewise, if you are writing a story of love between man and woman, it is worth bearing in mind that until quite recent centuries it was rare for young people of the landed classes to be allowed to marry by inclination; they were largely pawns in the game of 'empire building' practised by their parents, and few thought it anything out of the way, accepting as the norm the parental practice of starving or beating them into submission should they rebel. If they, then, fell in love, it was unlikely to be with the chosen spouse whom they had never seen before the nuptials and to whom they may well have been betrothed in their cradles.

The courtly love of which the minstrels sang, as exemplified by Lancelot and Guinevere or Tristan and Isolde, was inevitably directed toward some unattainable and therefore idealised love object. The idol of love either remained forever out of reach or fell from grace to consummation at the cost of mayhem and bloodshed.

The young of less elevated strata of society were more fortunate in that they, having less commercial value to their parents, were more free to marry for love-liking and spend their lives with whom they chose, even though it might be in a greater or lesser degree of poverty. But even at the level of the yeoman farmer, the merchant or the stapler, a certain amount of 'horse trading' with one's offspring was not unusual. A charming letter survives from a well-to-do adult, one Thomas Betson, to his twelve-year-old fiancée, Katherine, adjuring her to 'be a good eater of your meat alway, that ye may wax and grow fast to be a woman' ... and to 'greet well my horse and pray him to give you four of his years to help you withal. And I will at my coming home give him four of my years and four horse-loaves to make amends. Tell him I prayed him so ... '

He did not in fact marry her until she was fifteen, and as we might guess from the way he wrote to her, the marriage proved to be a happy one. But you have only to ponder the circumstances to glimpse a quite different story waiting to be written.

A wealth of such knowledge of family life, much of it gleaned from the famous Paston Letters, is to be found in G.M. Trevelyan's *English Social History*; if you can find the illustrated edition, so much the better. It gives a sound framework for every period from Chaucer's England to the 19th century, and makes an excellent nucleus for any historical library. You can then add more detailed studies of your chosen period, and will have a fair idea of what to look for.

It is of great advantage to build a reference library of your own; you will have your sources at hand for anything you need to verify, and if an editor challenges your knowledge, as may well be the case if you are an unknown writer, you can quickly find chapter and verse to settle the query.

You may feel it is an unnecessary expense to buy your own books, and there is no reason to think you have to acquire everything you see.

But if, as time goes on and you become more and more hooked on historicals, you merely buy what catches your eye as being of particular use, you will be surprised to see how quickly your shelves fill up.

If you can only afford to buy one book, look for something comprehensive which will give you a reliable framework over a broad spectrum. You can then, having selected your period, extend your knowledge in depth from other more specific sources.

Much has been said about the value of 'firsthand sources' in research, by which are meant documents in libraries and museums, often in obscure places and hard to find if you are writing, as you are likely to be, in your limited spare time. They are frequently difficult to decipher and also have to be looked up *in situ*, for which you are likely to need a special permit and probably an appointment. In either case, you will need unlimited time in which to find precisely what you need.

It is obvious that to the serious biographer such sources are essential and cannot be replaced by 'secondhand' sources, i.e. personal interpretations, however reliable, by other historians, since these will inevitably be coloured by the chroniclers' own views. But for the layman lacking the necessary expertise in translating early English, Italian or Old High German, or sufficient background knowledge to read them in the context of the times, it will be easier, if not safer, to ride on the shoulders of those who have gone before, and resort to the many excellent books of reference they have compiled. Look for the most recent, for new insights into history are constantly coming to light, and if possible read more than one writer's version in order to gain an unbiased view.

Many universities and other educational bodies offer weekend seminars on history. These are excellent, with tutors on hand who can help you with specific problems, and who are usually only too pleased to do so, recognising you as someone with a genuine interest. If you can find one of these seminars covering the period of your story you will be well advised to attend it.

Probably the most important thing to remember is what you are asking of your research, which is less how things appear to us now than how they felt to the people to whom it was all happening at the time.

Vital details can be gleaned in all kinds of ways. From costume books, which will tell you not only what the clothes, hairstyles, footwear and jewellery were like, both to look at and to wear, but why they were so designed. From herbals; even modern ones give useful information about the medicine practised by our ancestors. From books on country crafts and forgotten arts; it is in such publications that you will find the internal workings of such things as windmills and watermills, which you might otherwise have to travel hundreds of miles for the chance of seeing in action.

I once came across a recipe book for the foods we used to eat, and a 'coffee table' book, lavishly illustrated, on the English country house throughout the ages, which proved unexpectedly rich in the details of everyday life.

Do not despise school books. Nowadays they are extremely well researched and are designed to give an excellent overall picture of the life of the period.

Parish records and ancient gravestones yield a poignant story of birth, marriage and death in the recorded past, and of the often brief span of life in between. Never feel shy about asking questions. You will find that doors open as if by magic when you confide that you are writing a book. You will, of course, observe the courtesy of acknowledging such assistance when your work appears in print.

A visit to a historic house of the period can be of value in getting the feel of the time. Try to find a quiet corner, close your eyes and let the atmosphere of the past seep into you. I was once greatly helped by being able to go into a brewery attached to one of these houses, to actually see the layout of the vats and furnaces, and discover how home brewing was done in the Tudor age. In another, I found the shambles and kitchens preserved unaltered since the days of Elizabeth I.

Even in the runaway 20th century the student of history is still surrounded by such goldmines.

The list is endless. You have only to look about you.

Here, a word of warning: research is so fascinating to some writers (of whom I am one) that it can become obsessive. Beware of getting so carried away that you forget to write the book!

Beware of hindsight

If you mention an illness, do be careful not to impose a hindsight diagnosis which could not have been made in the relevant period. Most of the diseases people died of were known only by their symptoms, and while we may look back in our 20th century knowledge and recognise probable influenza or appendicitis we must remember that most ailments were lumped together under 'a fever', or 'the grippe', or even 'the sweating sickness'. The great Cardinal Wolsey died of what was known as 'a bloody flux', a symptom which might have been caused by almost anything. The plague of which we hear so much is known to have covered several forms which may well have been separate illnesses, the term 'plague' merely referring to any uncontrollable, fatal epidemic. There were certainly bubonic and pneumonic forms of plague, and the so-called Black Death which is now thought may have been the still deadly anthrax. The Red Death which swept Europe remains as mysterious today as it was to its victims.

Even the cause of death of King Henry VIII is still shrouded in doubt: it is known that he had a chronically ulcerated leg as the result of a riding accident; it is suspected that he was also syphilitic, and it is recorded that when his coffin was dropped it split open and gushed forth an evil-smelling fluid. But which of these things was directly responsible for his death is still a matter for surmise.

So don't feel that you have to name any illness your characters go down with. This is not to say, of course, that you should invent one! The important thing is to get the symptoms right, according to your own concept of what it was. Then leave your readers to speculate, as the unfortunate victims and those who tried to treat them had to do.

4
Characterisation

If you ask a gathering of people to think back to the book, play or even 'sit-com' they have enjoyed most, and then ask them to pinpoint what it is about it that they remember, the chances are that they will not come up with what happened during the course of the piece, but with one or more of the characters to whom it happened.

The conclusion is obvious: it is not the convolutions of the plot that stick in the mind, but the people involved in it. For the story to be remembered, those characters must be as real, as alive, as convincing as it is possible to make them, whether or not we as readers are expected to admire them. This applies not only to the central or 'sympathetic' characters, but equally to those who cross their path and foul up everything.

What this boils down to is the fact that you, as the writer, must know them thoroughly, must understand their follies and forgive their sins, whether of commission or omission. Bear in mind that every character we create is a reflection, however faint, of some element of ourselves; if it were not so we would be unable to predict their behaviour, and the story would be impossible to write.

It follows that you as their creator, their mother and father, must love them — which is not at all the same as having to like them. It means remembering that no one sets out to commit an evil deed for the sake of doing evil: there is always some reason, however distorted or perverted, which seems logical, right and justifiable to the doer.

A telling example of this appears in a modern short story by Anne Spillard, 'Love in the Third Age' which deals with an elderly couple where the man, although sliding into senility, is still being lovingly cared for by Addy, the common-law wife for whom he left his family in their youth. His middle-aged daughter takes advantage of his loss of orientation to snatch him back to live with her, ignoring the old woman and her feelings.

Her attitude is arrogant and insensitive, and in a couple of pages we have come to dislike her intensely. Until, her father having recovered a fragment of memory and wandered home to Addy, we find her sobbing 'I want my daddy ... I want my daddy!' and see through the behaviour to the little girl, the old unhealing wound.

No individual is all of a piece. There is good in the worst of us, and even the most exemplary have something we wouldn't like our friends to know about. Our inconsistencies are what make us human, and so it should be with fictional characters.

Beware in particular of making 'good' characters too good to be true. Watch for the heroine who is all sweetness and light, never loses her composure or has a bad mood; for the unreal hero who never loses a fight or fails to arrive like the cavalry at the precise moment when rescue is needed; for the villain who never makes a miscalculation and is only defeated by an amazing coincidence, or equally the one whose blunders are so stupid that we wonder how he manages to dress himself in the morning. They are all too unreal for us to identify with, and we will care very little what becomes of any of them.

A good plan is to make brief biographies of the two or three main characters before you start, to ensure that you know as much as possible about their backgrounds and past life. This will save a great deal of window gazing and pen chewing later on; it will also make certain that you do not lose sight of their ages, parentage and background with resultant contradictions in the text. If you form this habit, you will find that when peripheral characters begin to appear you will automatically ask yourself the same questions about them, which can only be to the good.

Be careful not to confuse your readers with too many characters of apparently equal 'weight', so that we don't know soon enough which one — or two — we should be watching for the main interest of the story. Avoid also the temptation, sometimes arising from research, of having characters, whether main or peripheral, with unpronounceable or equivocal names. These can prove such an irritation by causing a 'hiccup' every time we meet with them that the book may be put aside unread. Be warned.

Remember too the words of Robert Burns, 'Would to God the gift to gie us, to see ourselves as others see us.' Christopher Derrick, in his invaluable book *Reader's Report on the Writing of Novels*, explains it thus:

> Next time you see a couple of lovers, wholly wrapped up in each other upon a park bench, remember that there are no less than six characters present, and that they would all need to be taken into account if this apparently simple situation were to be wholly described. There's the man as he actually is, there's the girl as she actually is; there's his idea of her and her idea of him; there's his idea of himself and her idea of herself. Your novel contains more people than you suppose. ... And everything will be shifting and developing all the time.

This is particularly apposite when dealing with the generation gap, since parents and children in any age invariably see themselves and each other in entirely different lights. We have only to look within our own families to see that.

It also serves to remind us that to remain true to life, the characters must develop as the story progresses. If they do not, if they are not affected by what happens to them, either they or the plot are not valid and the whole thing fails to convince us. This is equally true of any form of fiction, whether it is a novel, a play or a short story.

In the short story, where the whole action will be encompassed in a brief timespan, perhaps a matter of hours, the incident of which you are telling us will be the pivotal point in a character's life, a crucial choice or a watershed which affects the future and, if well enough written, will also throw light on what has gone before to produce the situation.

In a play the time may be extended to cover a few weeks or months, in the case of a full-length stage production even longer, so that the writer has a little more latitude in deciding whether the action hinges on an incident or a phase in the character's life; but the same criterion will hold good.

A novel, on the other hand, generally takes the form of a journey or progression, e.g. from innocence to knowledge, from rags to riches, from ambition to downfall, or simply from the cradle to the grave which, in the historical context, must clearly show involvement in a particular crisis of the time. As the author, you have a special problem here. Having more time and space in which to work out your story, not to mention so much more knowledge to be held and organised in your mind, you may find it only too easy to forget that your characters will not emerge at the end of it exactly as they went in. The traumas – and the transports – they have experienced will have left their mark. This, after all, is how we grow up. Your characters must grow up too.

Having talked so far on general lines, let's look at some of the ways in which character can be shown.

Some writers like to describe the physical appearance of their main characters, while others prefer to leave such detail to the imagination to encourage reader identification, which might be less easy if we are told at the outset that he or she looks nothing at all like us. This is a decision which is entirely up to you, and it may be that your central character has some special physical peculiarity that we need to know about in order to understand the story, for example a witchmark, or a withered limb, fairly common in bygone times.

Here, a word of warning: if you do decide on a physical description (and this can be a useful introduction to secondary characters, seen as they are through the eyes of others), do it straight away. If you let us get halfway through, cherishing our own mental picture of a main character, and *then* tell us we have got it all wrong, it will not be appreciated!

On the whole, it may be of greater value to know what a person is like than how he looks. Here are some of the ways in which character is shown.

What we say   No two individuals, reporting on the same incident, will tell exactly the same tale. Each version will be coloured by the teller's own view of it and whether he or she is fairminded, emotionally biased or downright untruthful.

What we think   Often very different from what we choose to make public by saying it. This is particularly true of people on the brink of falling in love, who tend to approach one another 'back to back', fighting off the emotional intensity they have already foreseen.

What we do   This is fairly obvious but none the less important; our every action or reaction stems from the sort of person we are.

What we wear   This, especially in a historical context, will tell us much about social status and occupation, not to mention period, but be careful not to dwell on the subject too heavily and clumsily. Don't, for example, waste half a page in describing every detail of a costume when a passing reference to one key garment — a fichu, a farthingale, a coif — will do the job much better. How it is worn (carelessly or with meticulous concern for appearance, for example) tells us much more about the person wearing it.

What we like or dislike   This can distinguish the frivolous personality from the deep thinker, the depressive from the cheery soul. Think of people you know who cannot endure silence and feel compelled to fill it, while others need quiet and solitude in which to collect their thoughts. . . .

What we surround ourselves with   This ties in closely with the previous item. Stand in someone's living quarters and look around you, and you will learn a great deal about the occupant. You will know his or her taste in decor, in art (if any), whether it runs to reading and if so what kind of books, whether the owner is house proud and domesticated, or creative and bohemian, or perhaps an unusual combination of the one with the other . . . a liking for children or animals will probably be evident, a love of music or a passion for sport. . . . All these activities leave clues, and the information to be gleaned is most valuable. Standing behind someone at a supermarket checkout you can amuse yourself by trying to read character from what they buy.

There is also a rich harvest to be gleaned from looking into what is thrown away! Have a look in your own dustbin — are you a throw-away-and-start-again merchant, or a hoarder?

What we believe in – or don't Do your character's beliefs coincide with those of his contemporaries, or are we dealing with a potential rebel? This not only speaks volumes about the individual, but may be the very crux of your story.

What we eat and drink While what is eaten will largely be dictated by the period and financial status of the character, the way in which food is consumed will say much more about the individual. Is it bolted or savoured, does the quality or flavour matter or is quantity the main concern?

It has been said that the way we behave at table is the way we behave in bed. Think it over. . . .

How we sleep This can be significant. Someone who sleeps poorly is more likely to be nervous and highly strung than one who sleeps deeply and wakes refreshed.

There are of course many permutations on this theme, including the effects of guilt or worry on one who normally sleeps well; but all are useful in delineating character.

How we behave Timidly, or aggressively? And if the latter, does it cover basic insecurity or is it the sign of a selfish personality?

How we move Body language is one of the most useful ways of showing character. We have all met someone who 'talks with the hands', often a person with a lot to say who finds words inadequate. We have also seen the individual who hugs herself defensively (it is usually a woman), seemingly wanting to efface herself entirely. The way we stand, walk, sit, cross our knees or place the feet prosaically side by side, all have a tale to tell.

Body language can also be adapted to indicate mood, or response to another character, but it will always remain basically typical of the person concerned.

How we speak While this again will be governed to some extent by the period, the important thing from the characterisation point of view is the person's idiosyncrasies of speech. We all have them, although they will be more noticeable in some than in others. Dickens was well aware of this fact, and used it to good effect. That we all have favourite words and phrases which we use again and again will be only too obvious to the writer going through a typescript in search of his own repetitions! These speech patterns can be invaluable in establishing a character in the mind of the reader, but be careful. Don't get too carried away and impose the same one on *all* your characters, instead of just one, where it will do the most good.

The people we admire In other words, those whom we would most like to emulate, whether they suggest an 'improvement' on our own personality or fantasy figures. Either way, they are an indication of what we would like to be.

Those we despise   The significant point here is why we despise these people. Perhaps it is out of jealousy — they have more than we consider their fair share of life's advantages, or seem to have done less with what they had — or maybe they have transgressed against our particular code of ethics. The reason is what matters.

Those we wish to impress   We may want to impress for several reasons: we are ambitious and hope to catch the eye of somebody who might prove useful, or, having ourselves achieved success, we want to make sure it doesn't go unnoticed by those who haven't. Which it is will be dictated by the kind of person we are.

Those we want to outdo   The urge to outdo others may suggest a positive, fairly aggressive, perhaps even 'pushy' personality; equally it may show someone who is struggling gamely to match the success of another who has had more help on the way up. Which would it be for your character?

And not least, by our secrets   The things we keep hidden are the last to be discovered, and arguably the most significant of all. These are the things we are shy about; or, perhaps those we are ashamed of.

These are only some of the ways in which character is shown. Remember that it is also delineated by ambitions, fears, embarrassments, phobias — not exclusive to the 20th century, we can be sure — by dreams, which reach right down into the subconscious, by mannerisms and obsessions. The secretary of today whose desk is a miracle of obsessive tidiness is no different in essence from her ancestor who insisted on the pins withdrawn from her ruff being laid out in precise order on her dressing chest. Human traits change little over the course of centuries. It is merely our behaviour that is influenced by the mores of the times.

Finally, try to avoid artificial heroines of the type that seem to take off their crinolines and reach for the pill; bear in mind that until comparatively recently it was rare for sexual activity not to be followed by pregnancy, so you cannot afford to let women disport themselves too freely without their peccadilloes coming to light. Likewise, the man who received a wound in battle or in a duel was likely to suffer a long illness or lingering death as a result: no antibiotics then to take care of the danger of sepsis.

Know your characters thoroughly before you start. Remember not to tell us everything you know about them at once; never introduce them by means of the potted biographies you have written for your own reference or we as readers will get bored with waiting for the story to begin. Feed us the information little by little as the story progresses, and never put in anything just for the sake of it; in that way you will sustain our interest to the end.

5
Language and Dialogue

The first thing to be considered after characterisation is dialogue, and with it the language or 'voice' in which your story is to be told, which will probably be that of the main or 'viewpoint' character, the person whose story it is. So, before going any further, let us be quite sure we understand each other when we talk about the viewpoint.

Viewpoint

Broadly speaking, the viewpoint is the angle from which the story is told; the view through the eyes of the person whose story it is, through which all the other characters are seen. It is imperative to get right, for it is the 'voice' of the book — it must not be the author's voice, or the whole piece will have the impression of being told at arm's length, with no real involvement or reader identification. The best thing, especially for an inexperienced writer, is to go into one viewpoint, and stay there. Let me show you what I mean. Here is a short scene or passage in which the viewpoints are constantly changing:

> He smiled, but not because he felt like smiling. 'Just stop saying "Oh, Mark" and say you love me.'
> 'It's not as simple as that.' She felt the tears rising. To be offered the gift of love so late, so unsought ... and be afraid to take it. And she couldn't, not at the price ... she had to be wise for them both. 'I can't,' she said. 'Dear Mark, I can't. I only wish I could.'
> 'Explain to me!' Mark struggled to contain his bewilderment, his despair in the face of her finality.
> She shook her head. 'I can't explain, it's just — it would be wrong for you. And I know it would be wrong for me. I daren't, if you like.'
> Desperately he seized her hands. How could she just say no, and give him no reason ... 'Try me,' he pleaded. 'Just try to explain. You owe me that.'

The scene works, but only up to a point; something is missing.

We're not quite sure with which of them we should be sympathising, which is going to continue beyond this point – in fact, *whose story it really is*. This is because I have deliberately confused you by hopping from head to head, from one mind to the other and back again; something it is fatally easy to do unintentionally. Let's try it again, this time without the changes.

> He smiled, wanly. 'Just stop saying "Oh, Mark" and say you love me.'
> 'It's not as simple as that.' She felt the tears rising. To be offered the gift of love so late, so unsought ... and be afraid to take it. And she couldn't ... not at the price. She had to be wise for them both. 'I can't,' she said. 'Dear Mark, I can't. I only wish I could.'
> 'I don't understand,' said Mark. 'Explain to me.'
> 'I can't explain, it's just – it would be wrong for you. And I know it would be wrong for me. I daren't, if you like.'
> Mark took her hands. He looked miserable. 'Try me,' he said. 'Just try to explain. You owe me that.'
>
> (Extract from *Goodbye, Sally*)

You see the difference? We have stayed firmly in the woman's viewpoint by indicating only what she could *observe* of Mark's reactions, while giving her own in detail: his are still there, but by describing them *from the outside*, more subtly (and, incidentally, in fewer words) we are left in no doubt as to whose the story really is. It is the woman's. She is clearly seen as the central or 'viewpoint' character.

Don't, however, let me – or anyone else – bully you with so-called rules. You will no doubt be able to quote excellent writers who appear to take no notice whatsoever of rules and get away with it. But be in no doubt: when an expert breaks or ignores a rule, it is deliberate and to achieve a calculated effect. Once you have an equal understanding of the basics you will be able to do the same.

Characterisation and dialogue

Characterisation and dialogue are intimately related; dialogue is the very fingerprint of character, and it is also important that everything a character thinks, reflects on or remembers must be expressed in the language in which he speaks.

How then are you to differentiate successfully between characters, to make them easily distinguishable from one another and help us as readers to know which of them is speaking without your having to tell us with tedious repetitions of 'he said, she said', and the many variations which are even more obtrusive in the text? And how to avoid the commonest trap of all: finding that they all speak with one voice − your own!

Since they are all likely to be of the same historical period, think first of their environment, social status, age and occupation.

For example, a tough farmhand of the 16th or 17th centuries will not speak or think in the words of the learned man who tutors the sons of his employer, the lord of the Manor; words which you, as an educated writer, would find it natural to use. For one thing, being unlettered, he will have been unable to read or expand his vocabulary, and is very unlikely to have seen outside his own small community; for another, his nose will have been pressed too tightly against the grindstone to keep his children fed for any such notion to have entered his head. His thoughts may be just as profound as the tutor's but, being less articulate, he will find them much more difficult to express, and will have to fall back on similes drawn from his everyday life.

The landowner and his family will probably use a language different from either farmhand or tutor, a speech pattern affected by locality, upbringing, lifestyle and, not least, by the personal inclinations of each.

The speech and behaviour of men and women were more sharply differentiated in the past than they are today, which is something else to be borne in mind. Women were wise to be − or at least to appear − deferential to their lords and masters, who owned them like land or livestock or any other form of property, since only men could legally own money; the girl of independent spirit could only let off steam behind the scenes and often had to resort to underhanded methods to get her own way.

Here is a little exercise for you: spot the anachronism in the above paragraph, given that we were speaking of the 16th or 17th centuries. Having said which, let us look at the all-important question of suggesting period flavour.

In the 'Note' to her novel of the English Civil War, *They Were Defeated*, Rose Macaulay says: 'I have done my best to make no person in this novel use in conversation any words, phrases, or idioms that were not demonstrably in use at the time in which they lived.' She goes on to apologise to any who may feel that she has used 'too many words which now sound somewhat peculiar in our ears.'

This is a very delicate balance, essential to the smooth and pleasurable reading of any piece of historical fiction; on the one hand to avoid anachronisms, and on the other not to irritate your readers with too many pauses in which to wonder about, or be forced to look up, the meanings of the words you have used.

First, I would say to you beware of 'gadzookery,' by which is meant over-worked words like egad!, methinks, mayhap, zounds! and, of course, gadzooks! Not because these words don't belong to your period, they quite possibly do, but because they have been worn so thin by constant and sometimes careless use that they have become clichés in themselves. They have also been used to pepper stories which have relied on them alone to indicate a 'historical' content which, apart from the language, did not really exist.

Such a phrase as 'a manchet of bread' or 'pass the blackjack' not only tells us instantly that we are reading outside the present day, but does it far more deftly and effectively than any amount of gadzookery can do. You must, however, be sure to make clear from the context and within a few sentences the meaning of any word unfamiliar to modern ears. We readers are travelling in a strange land; don't leave us to puzzle over too-clever clues while you sail blithely on without us. Our enjoyment will be diminished, and we may even suspect that you are out to show us how clever you are.

On the subject of being clever, a timely word of caution.

The right word in the wrong place

Words change not only their usage but their meanings over long periods of time; some are more recent than we imagine, others much older than we might think. Such words as 'booze', for instance, and 'duds' (meaning clothes) which we might think of as modern slang have in fact come down to us from the thieves' cant of the 16th century, as has 'punk', which was synonymous with whore! Such words as 'char', 'thug' and 'bungalow' were unknown before the days of the Raj, having come to us via the Hindi language, while being 'clued up', which seems at first glance to be contemporary, actually comes from the sea-going lingo of the tall ships in the days of sail. Likewise, if we say today that a woman is honest, we mean that she is truthful, or not given to thieving; if we said it of her at an earlier period we would have been speaking of her chastity!

If, therefore, we fling such words about too freely without making sure that the reader understands their meaning in relation to the period, their usage will read like a mistake; the likely result is a challenge, from either an editor or a disbelieving reader who thinks you don't know what you are talking about!

Be wary, incidentally, of using 'thee' and 'thou', unless your characters happen to be Quakers, in which case it will serve to differentiate between them and others who are not. Used universally it can slow the reading and irritate the reader.

The question of how much or how little archaic language you

should use is one which only you can decide, having regard to your subject matter and the general style or 'voice' of the piece. Personally I use a very simple standard English for the narrative, and go through it with a fine-toothed comb at the editing stage in search of anything that could jar. While it might seem academically desirable to write as nearly as possible in the speech of the time, you have only to look up something written more than four or five centuries back to see that it would prove well nigh impossible to read for anyone untrained in translating — yes, it is just that — from Middle English. Chaucer provides us with a prime example.

In dialogue, a tiny turn of grammar, such as 'How like you that?' will give sufficient flavour without spoiling the flow. It is basically similar to writing in dialect: spelling it all out in detail will make it tedious to read, whereas a few key words or a change in the order in which they are spoken will indicate immediately the region the speaker comes from.

Having thought about the way to write dialogue, let us now consider its three main functions. They are:

To delineate character   I have already mentioned some of the ways of doing this. You will find many more of your own when you begin to write.

To convey information   This is a most useful device, often avoiding the need for a flashback (particularly tricky in the historical if you are not to confuse the reader; we shall deal with flashbacks separately later on), but it must be done subtly and naturally or it will stick out like a sore thumb. For example, if you have a wife reminding her husband of the ages or pursuits of their children, it will be only too obvious that the information has been 'planted' for the edification of the reader. The same goes for the passage of reminiscence in which the thinker uses the full names and/or occupations of those mentioned. An example might be:

> She thought back to the time when her husband, John Marriott, a
> captain in the King's army and an avowed loyalist, had attacked
> and wounded her brother James Sawyer, an honest man and
> among the most devoted of Cromwell's followers.

Can we really believe that she thought about this traumatic event in such cool and detailed terms? Finding that we can't will damage that 'willing suspension of disbelief' on which the storyteller depends; it will put us at arm's length from the character. Much more convincing would be something like the following:

She still found it hard to forgive John his bloody attack on James.
It was cruel enough that the man she had married should come
out on the side of the King, without the anguish of having to
stand by while he fought and wounded her brother.

The point here is not that the rest of the information, i.e. the reason
for the fight and the details of their names and affiliations, is not valid;
it is. But it does not belong at this point in the story. If we are part way
through the story we should have been told all this before; if it is in the
opening – incidentally, the most likely place for this kind of clumsiness
– there is all the more reason to be sparse with the information: tell us
just enough to whet the appetite, feed us only titbits. That is the way
to make us want to read on, to find out the rest.

To carry the story further   Every piece of dialogue should be a step
forward in the action. It may be the formation of a plan, a means of
introducing a new character, a piece of reportage of something vital
that has happened or is about to happen out of sight of the 'viewpoint'
character. Don't be beguiled by so-called rules which say that you must
have this or that percentage of dialogue to narrative in a well-
constructed book. The story itself will tell you where it is needed.
Never indulge in idle conversation for the sake of filling the page.

Many new writers encounter difficulties in the setting out of
dialogue, particularly in paragraphing. When it comes to indicating
who is speaking, good paragraphing is not only essential but obviates
many of the problems of 'he said, she said' mentioned earlier.

It has been said, and I'm sure it is true, that the simple 'said' goes
unnoticed by the reader, while contorted alternatives, (e.g. exclaimed,
cried, reposted, retorted, affirmed, alleged, asserted, stated, declared,
and – Heaven forbid – ejaculated!) found by diligent search through a
thesaurus, and used with the idea of relieving monotony, are far more
noticeable, and do nothing but cause a hitch in the reading by drawing
attention to themselves.

They do not really tell us anything material about the way in which
something is said, being mere variants of the same word, and the
manner of speaking will be obvious if the dialogue itself is couched in
the right words, and correctly paragraphed.

Here is an example of jumbled and confusing dialogue:

'Dunna do it, Tom.' 'I got to, you know I have.' 'But Margery –'
'There'll be others. It won't be so hard for her again. I'll make a
birthing stool so they come easy. You'll see, it's for the best –
better now than –' 'Tom ... what is it?' 'Witchmarked. Born dead.
Dunna look, I'll bury it outside.' 'It's not dead! Give it here! I

want my baby.' 'You canna do it, Tom. Here's your baby, dunna you fret yourself, 'tis a fine bonny girl. Only — 'tis witchmarked, like Tom says, and right bad. But we anna going to let him do away with it!' 'Oh, no! My baby — not my baby!' 'There! Now see what you done.'

As you see, it is difficult to tell who is speaking, or which of them is addressing whom, without a lot of irritating reading back and forth to find out. But give it paragraphing and intersperse it with a little action, and see the difference.

'Dunna do it, Tom!'

Tom's voice shook. 'I got to, Tib. You know I have.'

'But Margery —'

'There'll be others. It won't be so hard for her again. I'll make a birthing stool so they come easy. You'll see, it's for the best —' He spoke eagerly, trying to convince himself as much as her. 'Better now than —'

'Tom . . . ' a voice came feebly from the shadows. 'What is it?' After the months of waiting, the punishing hours of labour, was there a girl or a boy . . .

'Witchmarked.' Tom said it bluntly; the baby was quiet, so he added, 'Born dead. Dunna look. I'll bury it outside.'

'No, Tom!' Tibby snatched it from him and it set up a healthy cry.

'It's not dead!' Margery tried to struggle upright on the blood-soaked ruin of her bed, 'Give it here!' She reached out for it and then, bewildered by their reluctance, began to cry exhaustedly. 'I want my baby,' she begged weakly, pitifully.

'You canna do it, Tom!' Tibby put a stout arm about the weeping girl. 'Here's your baby, dunna you fret yourself, 'tis a fine bonny girl. Only — 'tis witchmarked, like Tom says, and right bad.' She glared fiercely in his direction. 'But we anna going to let him do away with it!'

'Oh, no!' sobbed Margery, her head bent over the puling infant. 'My baby — not my baby!' She rocked back and forth, hysterically clutching the child, and abruptly lost consciousness.

'There!' scolded Tibby, triumphant. 'Now see what you done!'

(Extract from *Gallows Wedding*)

Broadly speaking, a new paragraph is indicated when you move from one character, whether it be in word, thought or deed, to a different one. The reader then knows instinctively who you are talking about. The sequence above runs, Tibby, Tom, Tibby, Tom, Margery, Tom, Tibby, Margery, Tibby, Margery, Tibby. The reader has no problem in sorting out who is speaking, with not a 'he said/she said' anywhere. In case you should think me guilty of dissecting another writer's work let me explain that the above passage is from one of my own novels. As it formed a part of the opening, you will also find clues to the period in references to birthing stools, witchmarks and the primitive conditions of birth.

Another problem with dialogue can be uncertainty about how to use quotation marks, especially in dealing with the quote within a quote. Should they be double or single? And where exactly should they go?

Double or single quotes will be a matter of policy for the publisher to decide when it goes into print, but whichever you use in your typescript you must be consistent. If, for example, you choose to use double quotes for dialogue, i.e. at the beginning and end of each speech, you will employ single quotes for any reportage within that speech. For example, "He told me that they were going into battle the next day." But: "When I saw him he said, 'We go into battle tomorrow'." If you do this, don't forget to close *both* sets of quotation marks, sticking to the pattern in which you have used them.

One of the trickier aspects of dialogue is getting it to sound natural. In ordinary unstructured talk such as we exchange with family and friends, what we say is almost never a tidy exchange of question and answer; it is broken up into brief phrases which cross and intersect one another, often with more than one person speaking at a time (you have only to listen to an unscripted radio programme to realise this), continually subjected to interruption, and so ragged that it would be impossible to set it out on paper. The reason is that we are all more desirous of being heard than of hearing what another has to say! But how to make scripted dialogue seem natural is a question of careful balance between the pedantic recital of perfect sentences and the rough and tumble of everyday speech.

I have found it very useful to read my own dialogue aloud, either to myself or into a tape recorder, which I can play back later to a critical ear. This quickly shows up the flaws.

Another tip which you may find helpful if you are having trouble in getting the voice to match the character, is imagining that your story is about to be filmed, and selecting the actor or actress you would choose to play the part: then ask yourself if you can hear that actor speaking the lines you have given him.

One final word on the subject. When you have completed your work, sent it out and, we hope, had it accepted, you will find yourself faced, inevitably, with the publisher's requirements for editorial changes to the script. Usually these will be desirable, even though you may not agree at the time, and you will be well advised to make them.

In the case of dialogue, take a little extra care. It can happen that an over-conscientious copy editor will look at a speech containing, for example, 'I was sat sitting there,' and decide that it should be 'I was sitting there.' Grammatically, she will be quite right. But in altering it, she will have completely lost the regional flavour of the North of England from where the speaker comes, thereby weakening your careful work on the characterisation. If this happens, you should write back, pleasantly and diplomatically, explaining why you did it and asking for it to be changed back, and you will almost certainly find your original restored.

It always pays to query such details, politely and in a friendly manner — not as if you were out to look for trouble!

6
The Opening

Now that you have done your planning, have chosen your period, set up your theme, know your main characters and have a fair idea of where they are going, you are ready to start work.

Do I hear you breathe 'at last'? Well, I know it's a long frustrating wait to see those first few words shining on the paper, but the truth is that if you haven't done enough forward planning, you are likely to run out of steam after the first few pages.

On the other hand, you may be muttering 'Yes, but how do I start?' This is a vital question; on it will depend very largely the success of your book.

The short answer is: by going straight into the action. What the reader wants at this stage is involvement; the rest can follow. So start with people rather than with descriptions, with dialogue rather than with wordy introductions. Go, not from the general to the particular, but from the particular, that is the main characters, to the general. Many successful writers start with dialogue, then briefly step aside to put us in the picture before turning to more dialogue, thus getting the story moving from the very first word.

A good, arresting opening is all-important. It is the shop window of your work, the first thing that anyone sees, be it agent, editor, publisher or browser on the bookstall. Ideally, it will tell us who, why, where and when, although not necessarily in that order.

The primary functions of an opening are discussed in the next few sections.

Setting the period

Unless your story is set in a time so remote, or so exotic, that the necessary clues would take up such an unwarranted share of our attention that we give up and try reading something else, it is better to avoid setting the period by merely stating the date. It is in any case a clumsy, rather lazy way of achieving your aim, and may tempt you to think that having done so you don't need to take the trouble of describing the scene.

This is a misconception. The reader may have very little grasp of the way people lived in that particular year, and will need more help in creating the backdrop against which your story is to be played out. In addition to this, the bald setting of dates can have the added drawback of giving the impression of a textbook and putting the reader off it altogether.

Briefly, if you really feel the setting demands a date, make sure you sketch in the mental picture as well.

Sketching is the word to hold on to at this stage. As we saw with regard to both costume and dialogue, a few key items mentioned in passing are all that is needed: the form of lighting, be it candles, rushlight, oil lamps or gaslight, will assist greatly in setting the period, as will a subtle reference to the type of chair on which someone sits, or the fact that there is glass, vellum, oiled paper or nothing at all in the window – you will no doubt think of equally effective ways of your own.

The great thing is the creation of atmosphere. This can be done best by the use of all the senses; don't stop at telling us what is to be seen, think of the smells, some of them so insistent that they can almost be tasted. These are very evocative; every time and place has its characteristic smell, the pitchfires burning on street corners during the Plague of London, the animal odours haunting medieval homes which housed livestock in the 'undercroft' below, while their human owners slumbered overhead, the unforgettable odours of woodsmoke, gunpowder and burning flesh while martyrs were burnt alive. Tell us what we can hear, whether it be the church bell, the oxen lowing, the geese cackling, the post horn, or the grinding of iron-shod cartwheels over cobbles or whatever the road surface was at that time.

Touch a piece of homespun, or sacking, or handmade lace, to discover its texture and convey it to us. Then you will have gripped our attention; you will have shown us the time and place, instead of boringly telling us. It is all done by mirrors: you hold up the mirror to the times, we look into it and are fascinated by what we see. We want to go further with you – and your battle is half won.

Before you get too carried away, a word of warning: even your best descriptions shouldn't be included as huge indigestible chunks. Description is far more effective – and acceptable – if fed in little by little, as small delicious 'tasters', and passing references as the story moves. It must never be allowed to clog the action, and the very worst place this can happen is in the opening scenes.

Establish the main character/s

Never try to introduce all the characters on the first page. The one you must introduce, and closely involve us with, is the central character;

the one whose story we are about to hear. By now, if you have done your homework, you will know very clearly who this is. It is possible that you have decided to share the honours between two, or more, in which case, unless you are already an experienced writer, you will be running into problems over viewpoint.

You may choose to tell the tale exclusively through one character's eyes, as in the personal narrative or 'I' style. This has certain advantages in that reader involvement is most easily achieved and held; it has the disadvantage that anything happening out of sight of that character cannot be personally witnessed but must be related by someone else, which may involve a certain loss of drama. But it can be done.

If you decide to use one exclusive viewpoint without putting it into the personal 'I', but using the more usual third-person singular, you have a little more latitude, in that you can occasionally switch to the eyes of another character who is equally involved to show us something that we need to know about, of which the main character has to remain ignorant.

You may want to divide your story between three or even four people in order to show it from different angles. This too can be done, although it is not the easiest way and you will need some expertise to get away with it.

The fact is that you can do anything you like *as long as you do it well enough.* What you must not be tempted to do is constantly switch from one viewpoint to another indiscriminately; if you do, you will confuse us so totally that we no longer know – or care – who we are reading about. And once we cease to care, you have lost us.

To sum up: you will be wise to avoid any change of viewpoint on the first page, and preferably not in the first chapter.

Suggest the theme

The opening should give a flavour of the kind of book it is, and what it is about. After one or two pages at most, we'll want to know whether to expect comedy, tragedy, something deeply reflective, a near documentary with strong political overtones or a piece of light entertainment which is meant to be taken purely for fun. If you start in one mood and then veer off into something entirely different, we may feel cheated as we read on or even decline to finish it. And it is unlikely that a publisher would take it anyway.

Trigger the action

This is largely a matter of deciding where to start. The best place is just
before some dramatic crisis is reached, a crisis which will pinpoint the
conflict which makes a situation into a story. Don't be tempted to start
too soon. If we come to your house for a meal, we don't want to wait
in the kitchen watching you prepare the vegetables, wash the meat,
chill the wine and set the table while the roast takes its time in the
oven; we want to arrive when it it almost ready. If we have only been
invited for a cup of tea we are not interested in watching you fill the
kettle, wash up the cups and wait for the milk to be delivered. We want
to arrive at the point *just before the kettle boils*, when something
interesting is just about to happen. And that is the place to start your
tale.

Engage the reader's curiosity

Don't tell us everything too soon. Arouse our curiosity by suggesting
what may be about to happen, but don't tell us what it is before we get
there. Tempt us to follow you with titbits, hints of what is to come; we
will follow you like stray dogs hoping for a feast. Every story needs
some degree of suspense, whether it is life or death or merely a
question of 'will she, won't she?' which is answered on the last page. If
you telegraph that answer we may feel that reading the rest would be a
waste of time.

In short, aim for a beginning that will do all these things, without
the stitches showing. Mary Webb did it beautifully in the opening of
Precious Bane. Who could fail to be captivated by this:

> It was at a love-spinning that I saw Kester first. And if, in these
> new-fangled days, when strange inventions crowd upon us, when
> I hear tell there is even a machine coming into use in some parts
> of the country for reaping and mowing, if those who mayhappen
> will read this don't know what a love-spinning was, they shall
> hear in good time.'

Note how subtly the information is offered; we have met both the
main characters, know already that the viewpoint is the speaker's, that
she is a countrywoman, probably of farming stock, and is living before
the days of mechanised farming or factory-made fabrics. And all in the
space of two sentences, one little paragraph.

In her foreword the author says: 'To conjure, even for a moment, the
wistfulness which is the past is like trying to gather in one's arms the
hyacinthine colour of the distance. But if it is once achieved, what
sweetness! — like the gentle, fugitive fragrance of spring flowers, dried
with bergamot and bay.'

Small wonder that *Precious Bane* has become a classic. If you have not yet read it, you have a great pleasure to look forward to.

We have only talked so far about the main characters. There will be others coming into the story, but you need not introduce them yet, indeed would be wise not to do so until they have something relevant to do. When they do appear, they will be seen through the eyes of the central character and this is where a physical description is both helpful and suitable, because it so often figures in a first impression. Be careful not to tell us things about them that your character would not know, slipping out of the main viewpoint and destroying the illusion of reality. You have probably already named them for yourself, so be careful not to tell us those names before they are known to your viewpoint character.

Remember that names, like anything else, go in and out of fashion over the years; you would not for instance find a Darren or a Marlene outside the 20th century (although clearly that is an extreme case), and it is worth bearing in mind that names, especially surnames, often went with occupations. You would be unlikely, for example, to find a Smith as a farmer in, say, mediaeval times, or a Cooper making his livelihood baking pies. Work often ran in families, fathers passing on their skills to their sons, and before the great migration to the cities, cottages were passed down from hand to hand in the same way. It was nothing unusual for country people to live and die in the same village without ever venturing outside it.

Back to openings. In writing drama it is worth remembering that the first few minutes of a play are often lost. In a theatre, someone will inevitably come in late and disturb a whole row of other people; at home, watching television or listening to a radio play, your audience will be even less captive — the telephone or the doorbell may ring, or the child upstairs choose this precise moment to ask for a drink, and the vital opening lines will have fallen on deaf ears. Yet, if interest is not captured at the outset, the on/off switch is all too readily available — so what is the answer?

Obviously you must have the atmosphere, the tension, the sense of something about to happen which is not to be missed; broadly speaking, all the above advice holds good. But you will be wise to avoid having anything crucial actually happening in the first few minutes. Give yourself a little more time — but only a little — to set up the situation. Then plunge straight in.

Finally, openings of any kind are notoriously difficult, carrying as they do so much responsibility. Great writers have had problems with them before us; did you know that Tolstoy's *Anna Karenina* begins at what was originally Chapter Three? It is sometimes impossible to find the right opening before the rest of the story is told.

If you find yourself terminally stuck with yours, put it behind you and plough on. I have known people to get so bogged down that they never got further than Chapter One, going back over it again and again, trying fruitlessly to perfect it. Don't beat your brains out over it. Carry on with the story, get it all down on paper, and then come back to the opening when you have completed your first draft. The chances are that you will know exactly what is needed, once you can see it in context with the rest. Writing is a little like climbing: once you have started, don't look down until you reach the top.

7
Keeping the Pages Turning

It is all too common, having put so much into creating a masterly opening, to feel uncertain how to move on to the next stage. It is also dangerously tempting to think that the rest will be easy because the main effort is behind you. The latter is palpably untrue, as you will quickly find out.

Dramatic content

If you have problems getting beyond the opening it may be that you have chosen to begin with the most dramatic event of the book. When this is the case, the remainder of the story is doomed to anti-climax. You will have created a brilliant opening – but you have left yourself nowhere to go. Ideally, a story should progress through a series of dramatic peaks, the strongest being kept for the end. In this way, the suspense can be built up gradually during the reader's voyage of discovery in a way that rivets attention to the last page. If you have used the highest dramatic peak too soon, you will have scuttled the ship before it has left the harbour.

By all means look for an unusual and dramatic situation on which to raise the curtain, but be sure that you can not only follow it but better it. The conflict should increase thereafter, not diminish, or the story will inevitably run downhill. One publisher, asked why she would not judge a manuscript on the three chapters and a synopsis which new writers sometimes submit, replied: 'If you had seen as many novels as I have, which start brilliantly and then disappear into the sand, you would not ask.'

Conflict and suspense

As we have seen, an element of suspense is vital to any story. If you can produce a story in which the resolution of one crisis results logically and inevitably in the setting up of the next, so much the better. Your character, having sought and found a path leading out of trouble, finds that as a result a worse disaster looms ahead.

Let us for a moment go back to our Royalist wife with her Cromwellian brother. We will suppose that she has concealed and secretly tended her wounded brother, thereby saving his life: resolution of crisis number one. But now comes the conflict: she discovers that her compassionate action has placed her unwitting (and still loved) husband under the charge of treason by succouring an enemy of the King. He will suffer disgrace and disaster unless she can find a way to avert them.

A cliché situation perhaps, but one which serves to illustrate the point: here we have the embryo of crisis number two, and therein lies the suspense.

The 'chapter-hook'

This is the most effective point at which to make the chapter break: the point at which the reader cannot put it down without reading on to find out what will happen. A chapter that ends too cosily, with its problems neatly solved, can be set down by the reader and returned to at leisure; in a busy life, this may mean not at all. Ending each chapter just as the new crisis threatens, in other words on a 'cliffhanger' (a phrase borrowed from the early cinematic serials) will ensure that the next chapter is started, and the next and so on until the final dénouement. This does not mean that every chapter has to end with frantic activity or violence; a question in the reader's mind will be enough to sustain suspense. But there must be something; not for nothing is it called a 'chapter hook'.

The ending

It is by no means easy to decide exactly where a story should end. Should it wind down gently, tying up all the loose ends from earlier in the tale, thus making sure that the reader knows the answers to every possible question, spread over the last two, three or even more pages? Should it end abruptly with a bang, leaving all else up in the air? Should it leave the reader to work out the answers, perhaps with a sense of anti-climax and dissatisfaction?

In each of these examples there is an inherent flaw.

The first approach can lead to tedious overexplanation and ruin the impact unless it is done by a very experienced hand. It can be avoided by ensuring that all the really relevant questions have been answered before the final page, leaving a way open to the combination of impact with inevitability that characterises a really good ending. This is particularly so in the big historical adventure.

On the other hand the 'big bang' can leave the reader frustrated and disappointed in quite another way. The third method has more going for it, but only if you can be quite confident that you have given all the clues needed; it is too easy to think that we know as much as you do — and we may not. With no dramatic climax to tell us that it is over we may even start looking for a missing last page.

The choice, of course, is yours. What you must never do is throw in the towel and solve everything by means of an amazing coincidence. We all know that such things happen in real life but you are writing fiction. If you offer us the kind of solution which makes us scoff, 'Tell us another one!', we will quite simply refuse to accept it. So will a publisher.

In this, as in everything, only you can decide, whether by balanced judgement or an educated guess; it is largely a matter of judiciously choosing your moment. Logically, the place to end is *where the rest of the story can be foreseen.*

This is only possible if you have tied up the loose ends beforehand, or at least have predicted what they are likely to be. A good ending, whether happy, tragic, or poignant, has a duty to satisfy your readers; to leave us, whether or not we have been caught by surprise, with the realisation on reflection that whatever happened was the only possible thing. To leave us, whether laughing or wistful, at least satisfied.

Having moved rather swiftly from opening to ending, let us consider some of the problems confronting you in between.

Accuracy v. entertainment

For the historian this question presents no problem: above all else he is the chronicler, the seeker after truth. Accuracy must remain paramount, and the entertainment content of his writing must come either from a sparkling and witty style, or from some completely new knowledge of his subject. On no grounds can he allow himself to distort the facts.

You on the other hand, as a writer of fiction, may find yourself faced with a dilemma. Perhaps you have reached a situation where you wish to make use of a true event, but the story would only work if it had taken place elsewhere, or at another date.

This can be quite a problem: are you to sacrifice a really exciting and dramatic scene in the interests of accuracy, or defy history and hope that no one will notice? This is a situation which must have confronted the makers of the film *Witchfinder General*, the story of which was based on the life of the notorious Matthew Hopkins; to increase the excitement, suspected witches were shown as being barbarously flung into the flames, whereas in fact the penalty for witchcraft *in England* at the time was not burning but hanging, the fate of burning at the stake being reserved for heretics. A witch would therefore have been burned only if she had 'worked witchcraft against her husband', the killing of a husband (though not, you will note, of a wife!) being classified as heresy, since it went against the teaching of the church. This does not appear to have bothered either producers or audience, who were solely concerned with entertainment, and certainly did no harm at the box office. But can we be confident that the readers of novels – particularly historicals, which are often read by those with a special interest in the period – are going to be as indulgent?

This is a question to which you must find your own answer; but be assured that if you make a deliberate error, there will always be someone who will know better and write to you – even if, as is unlikely, your editor doesn't suss you out first! So don't rely on getting away with it.

Your best resort is to re-think your position; adjust your plot to accommodate the facts, not the other way about. A good guideline to follow is this: extrapolate on history if you can, stretch it if you must, but don't distort it and never resort to lies.

Supplementing the dialogue

If you have involved in your story real people who are known to have lived at the time, you will undoubtedly come up against the question of what they would say in a given situation. What if no speech has been recorded, as will certainly be the case if that situation is one which you yourself have invented for them?

When this question was put to historical biographer Jasper Ridley, he gave as his opinion that it was permissible to invent dialogue for such characters, *provided* that an author had researched the original people to the point of understanding them, so that any 'invented' dialogue would remain in keeping with their known character and personality.

If you don't feel confident to do this, you will be wise to use such personages as window dressing, and keep them firmly in the background where they will be seen and not heard.

Needless to say, the same rule must apply to their behaviour. Who would be convinced to read of the austere Henry VII surrounding himself with artists, poets and musicians and revelling in the latest dances as did his grand-daughter Elizabeth I? It would fly in the face of what we already understand of his character. Which brings us back to that iceberg of unseen but vital research.

The angle of presentation

If you have decided to speculate on the life of some minor figure of history (you will be wise to avoid the very well-known as they are already over-written), presenting it as fiction, or 'faction' to use a recently coined word, then 'history through the keyhole' can be an intriguing way of telling a tale of the great or famous. This allows you scope but without venturing too far into a minefield of guesswork as to private feelings and motivation. It is achieved by telling the tale through wholly fictional characters, domestics or liegemen, or perhaps dependent relatives, who will also provide a sub-plot of their own, not only to add interest but to illustrate how the lives of the powerful inevitably affect those of the underlings. If you use the observer as your viewpoint character you will lose nothing of drama or emotional involvement, for these will be conveyed through that character's personal reactions.

Obviously this method needs careful handling; a good trick, as the saying goes, if you can pull it off.

Sex and violence

It seems to me a pity that sex and violence are so often lumped together as though they were synonymous, or at any rate inseparable.

So let us take violence first. How much should you include, and how best to handle it?

It is possible that past ages tended to be more violent than the present, although many would disagree. It may be merely that, in the absence of media titillation, it was taken more for granted. Be that as it may, it is certain that in a story of battles or uprisings, of piracy at sea or the colonisation of the Americas, a degree of violence is essential to the action. A degree of violence, enough and no more, to lend realism, conviction and, let it be admitted, excitement to the narrative. What it *is* desirable to avoid is that extra helping, artificially added like food colourings, to shore up a wilting plot. Where violence is needed, describe it honestly; pull no punches and be as truthful as you can, being careful to avoid the use of violence for its own sake, dressed up as 'good, clean fun' with no resultant suffering.

Where it is not needed, leave it out. It will never be missed.

Much of the above can be applied equally to dealing with sexual scenes. These are some of the most difficult scenes to handle well, and give rise to many a headache. Some writers would prefer to leave them out altogether, but this is too easy an option. If, for instance, your story carries a strong love theme, which can give extra life and warmth to the most serious piece of writing, we, your readers, may feel disappointed or even cheated if, having carried us to the bedroom door, you slam it in our faces. We are only human, we have a natural curiosity and already you will have evoked in us a degree of concern for the lovers whose fortunes we have followed so far: we should like to know if the affair is consummated, and if so whether in ecstasy, quiet contentment or in such a disastrous fiasco that the whole relationship shivers.

Describe your love scenes honestly, if you're going to do it at all. Concentrate on emotion and sensation, rather than on clinical detail, of which we are all aware anyway, and which becomes boringly repetitive after a very short span (one of the problems encountered in second and subsequent novels is how to describe the sexual act yet again without saying the same old thing). Try to write them so well that the reader enjoys them, perhaps is treated to a little glow, without your having had to resort to inexpert pornography.

The late John Braine once said, 'Surprise your reader; shock him if you like, but please don't disgust him.' You couldn't have better advice, whatever the period of the piece.

8
Structure and Working Methods

The questions writers are most often asked must be: how do you work? Do you plan your time/write longhand or straight on to the typewriter/use a word processor/set yourself a daily word stint/work nine to five or ... stop! Just stop right there.

The fact is, there are as many ways of writing as there are writers. One very successful novelist of my acquaintance used to complete one chapter every morning before breakfast, edit it in the evening after work and then go on to the next the following morning, never looking back or needing to do another draft. Another, equally successful, does not touch the typewriter for weeks and then works ten to fourteen hours at a stretch, being able to cut herself off completely from daily life during that time. Others find they have to fit in a few minutes here and there, but keep the story running in the mind while the hands are occupied with other things.

One thing is sure: you should never wait for the perfect circumstances in which to start your writing. They will never come, and you will find yourself in old age looking back on the writer you might have been. The chances are that you will never attain that ideal state of being able to write all day with no interruptions; few people ever do, and certainly not while learning the craft. You can only operate in the circumstances you have; use them, bend them if necessary, but start now. You may well find that your social life suffers, the friends you had become a little thin on the ground. But you will make new friends through writing, the more rewarding in that they will understand if you have to go into retreat from time to time, simply because they share your problems, and your burning interest. You will be able to talk to them about your work without their eyes glazing over with lack of comprehension.

Whether you write longhand or into a machine matters nothing at all; find the way that suits you and use it, taking no notice of what other writers do. Above all, don't be intimidated by the feats of writers more prolific. Perhaps they did write a bestseller in six weeks, while you are still struggling with Chapter Ten after six years. When yours hits the bookstalls, who is going to know — or care? It will be all the better for the extra time and care you have put into it. Don't be panicked into rushing it.

Historicals are demonstrably longer than contemporary novels, and will naturally take longer to complete. Besides which, they need time for research, for checking, for writing and rewriting until they reach the necessary high standard. Slow writers can console themselves with Aesop's fable of the vixen and the lioness, who met for the first time after both had given birth.

The vixen, full of herself, was boasting to the lioness of the many beautiful cubs she had produced, adding a little patronisingly, 'And how many did you have, my dear?'

'Just one,' purred the lioness. 'But that one is a lion.'

Targets v. deadlines

We all have a common enemy: laziness. I have often suspected that some of those who do write rapidly do so in order to get back to doing nothing as soon as possible! And there is nothing wrong with setting yourself a target, once you have started to write in earnest.

A target, you will note, not a deadline. Unless you are one of those who need a quick panic to goad you into working, you may find as I do that deadlines scatter your wits when writing fiction, and never more so than when tackling a big historical. If you do, by chance, find yourself obliged to accept one, try to have it set by negotiation with the publisher; think of the time in which you think you can deliver, *and then double it*. Then, work to the date you first thought of.

There is nothing dishonest in doing this. By such an arrangement, you will be sure of delivering on time or even before, your publisher will love you, and you will have given yourself leeway, time to stand back from your draft, to cut and polish it until it represents your best work, and a chance to cope with the interruptions that will inevitably beset you at that frantic last minute. It will also allow for delays, the dreaded writer's block, time lost through flu or other emergencies, and those 'can-you-just' jobs that non-writers press upon you at the worst possible moment.

Back to targets. Only you know your own circumstances, and it would be invidious for me to suggest a work schedule to suit you. However, a useful formula in general terms is to consider a date when you would like to have the work finished, and roughly how many thousand words long you think it is likely to be; then you can work out how much work you need to do per day to achieve it.

Calculating wordage

You can work out the number of pages in relation to wordage by the following method: first count the number of words in your line of typing (probably about ten) and take an average over ten lines. Multiply this figure by the number of lines on the page, let us say thirty, and you will know how many words per page you are producing, on this calculation 300 to 350. Divide your total length by this number and you will know roughly how many of your pages will be needed to complete the first draft. You can then work out the ratio of pages to days according to your personal working pace to arrive at a probable completion date.

Don't be daunted if the estimate turns out to be impracticable in your given circumstances. Simply set your completion date further ahead, and don't worry if it looks like taking years; it probably will, and be none the worse for that. It is infinitely preferable to skimping the work. Even when it seems to be finished, that is to say, all on paper in black and white, you will certainly want time to edit and improve, perhaps even to re-write a second or even a third draft before you are satisfied. It has been said with great wisdom that if you want your work to be read more than once, you must be prepared to write it more than once, and if I could select just one piece of advice to leave you, I think that is what it would be.

Beware of setting yourself a target so unrealistic that you are courting failure and frustration. It may be better to set yourself a weekly, rather than a daily stint, whether it be in wordage or hours worked, and to let it be reasonable and within the bounds of your daily life. If you do this, you need not panic if on one day you are ill, or have to be away from home: you will be able to make it up on another day and still meet your target. The pages will tick up nicely, the work keep its continuity.

If you have rashly accepted a publisher's deadline without sufficient forethought, reverse the calculation. Start with the delivery date, look at the length of the work (you will have agreed this in the contract), and divide the total number of (your) pages needed by the number of working days left. When you have worked out this simple formula, come hell or high water you must stick to it if you are to meet the deadline.

Writer's block

Breaking the thread of what you are writing for too long at a time is a prime cause of the dreaded 'writer's block'. The longer you are away from it, the further you drift, and the harder it becomes to get back into that world from which you have wandered. If this should happen, your best resort may be to read back over what you have already done, edit it and improve on it, and with luck you will find yourself going on from the point where you left off.

Since we have mentioned writer's block, we may as well go on to consider some of the other causes. First let us differentiate between the normal daily reluctance that afflicts us all and is fairly easily dealt with by the method outlined above, and the classic, crippling, clinical type that can seize us up as solidly as an engine that has blown its main gasket.

One, as you may have guessed, is the acceptance of a too-short deadline, which looms terrifyingly ahead like an oncoming train, blotting everything else from your mind. Prevention is a whole lot easier than cure. Try to avoid the deadline before you start; if it is too late for this, telephone your editor and plead for an extension. If he or she proves adamant, remind yourself that you can invent an illness to cover your late delivery — anything to release the tensions that are making it impossible to write. The chances are that you will make the deadline as promised, once you have removed the element of panic.

Another cause is that you may have relied too heavily on the period for the interest of the piece, with the result that having painted the picture, however well, you are unable to think of what your characters can do next. An indication of this is when, having drawn a blank, you decide that perhaps a bit more research will give you an idea. The real trouble is that either you have lost sight of your theme, or you fell into the trap of starting without one. There is also a fair chance that you have been writing about the period, rather than the people.

In this too, prevention is better than cure; if you haven't spent sufficient time on planning, you will have to go back to that stage before you can move on. Once you really know what your theme is, and where your characters are going, you will be able to see ahead.

You may be held up for a piece of information without which you can go no further, and which you have so far been unable to trace. Perhaps, for example, as I did during the writing of my first historical, *Gallows Wedding*, you foresee a trial looming on the horizon, and while knowing that it has to take place not in the Star Chamber but in the manorial or 'court leet', still be unable to find enough details of procedure. I was stuck for several months at this hurdle — until it occurred to me to make the chapter break on the arrest, and pick up the narrative in the next one after sentence had been passed. The actual trial was not needed, and in fact was never missed! However, only desperate straits call for desperate measures, and it is best to have everything at your fingertips if you can.

Another possibility is that you have painted yourself into a corner, having sewn up your protagonists so tightly that you can find no possible way out. Either they have reached the end of the road, in which case you will be within a few pages of the end, or they have wilfully shot off up a blind alley from which they can't be extricated.

If this has happened at an early stage, you have some thinking to do. You may have to go back over your narrative and unobtrusively unpick a few stitches in order to give them an escape route and a chance of surviving to the end. Again, sufficient forward thinking at the beginning would have avoided the necessity of rescue at a later stage.

In a nutshell, the answer to most forms of writer's block lies in the causes. If you find yourself stuck, examine your priorities and motivation, and check your theme.

Keeping an eye on the time

Time scale can be considered from two angles: one is the avoidance of perpetual summer, two-year winters and elephantine pregnancies. In other words, making sure that the lady who was sweet and twenty at the beginning of a lengthy war is not still twenty — however sweet — at the close. This may sound absurd, but you may be surprised how easily it can happen. Children must be allowed to grow up; if there are several involved, make sure they do so at the same rate — don't slip up by letting the younger sister in Chapter One become the elder in Chapter Seven! The baby born in Chapter One may well be walking by Chapter Three, and who knows what he may be up to by Chapter Ten.

Old age and even death must be allowed to overtake, if the timescale is long and your characters are to be real to us. As the months pass, remember to let the seasons change; check on such matters as someone saying, 'We must go now, before the roads become impassable', and someone else in the same scene mentioning that the roses or the buttercups are in bloom. It can happen. . . .

In another sense, keeping an eye on the time relates to the chronology of the action. It is not necessary to show every boring minute of the progress. Remember that fiction is life with the dull bits cut out. Never think you can rely on the methods of the 19th-century classics to carry you through; in the changing years since the great Sir Walter Scott, we readers have become spoilt children, we only want the interesting bits. If you force us to wade through page after page in search of what we want, we may give up.

So if a week, or a month, or a year has passed with nothing particular happening, leave it out. Break off your narrative and pick it up when the next kettle is ready to come to the boil. If it is within a matter of hours, this can be done by means of a double line space within a chapter. It is not even necessary to tell us that time has passed; the fact that the location has changed is enough to indicate it. Suppose that the previous scene has ended in a garden, with the sun shining. You could start your next scene thus, after a double line space:

Amelia set down her embroidery upon the lamplit table and looked across at her husband.

We instantly know that not only has the scene changed, but time has moved on. If we are taken into the presence of two characters who did not appear in the last scene, their names alone will suffice; the rest is simple.

Here we can refer back to the change of season. If we are transported from winter to summer it is obvious that at least half a year has passed, and in this case it may be desirable to start a new chapter, certainly if the time difference is a matter of years.

That is all very well, you may be saying to yourself, but how am I supposed to fill in the one or two things that happened in the interim?

There are various ways of doing this. You can do it by reference during a narrative passage (that is, where you are giving information in the text); you can have the missing event referred to in dialogue, being watchful not to have the speaker fill it in too obviously. Or, as a last resort, you can do it by means of a flashback in someone's reverie.

The flashback

Note well: as a last resort. This is because flashbacks are notorious invitations to confusion, and never more so than in the historical. We as readers may have only just got ourselves orientated to the particular time in which the piece is set, when we are suddenly transported to another and expected to keep up. It is asking too much of us.

So, if you do find a flashback is unavoidable – and the flashback is by no means to be despised – make sure that you have framed it clearly, and don't do it more than once or at most twice, in the length of a story. A historical that jumps back and forth throughout its length is at best confusing and at worst unreadable.

A word on exactly what is meant by 'framing': it is the isolation of the flashback so that it doesn't read like a part of the current action. Since it will inevitably take place in someone's memory, the 'frame' can be achieved by describing that character in a definite situation (either performing some activity or looking at something which has evoked the memory) and then at the end of the flashback returning very clearly to that same scene or activity, so that we know we are again with the character's 'present time'.

Should you phrase the whole of the flashback in the pluperfect tense, i.e. had had, had gone, had wanted to? Not, for choice, the whole of it, or it will seem pedantic and be irritating to read. What works best is to start it in that tense for the first sentence or so, then revert to the ordinary past tense until the final sentence, and then revert to the pluperfect for those final words. You will then have made it perfectly clear that the flashback is over, and can return to the normal past tense in restoring the thinker to his or her previous occupation.

An example might be:

> From where she stood by the window she could see the moonlit gazebo where she and Johannus had held such passionate rendezvous that summer. She pleading, always pleading, and he adamant. . . .
> 'Why must you go, surely there are others.'
> 'And I am of their number.' Was the afterglow in his eyes already chilling? 'Honour forbids that I should turn my coat.'
> She would not allow herself to weep, to mar their few precious moments together with tears. She only whispered, 'And what of me?'
> He had drawn her again into his arms. 'Your valour lies in waiting, as mine on the field.'
> Was it really only three years since . . . so much had happened, birth and death in the countryside torn by war. But Johannus had gone with the rest to defend his beliefs, and had never returned . . . only a scribbled message on a bloodstained scrap of parchment. A message of love, of remembrance; she had it still . . .
> She cleared her eyes, turned abruptly back towards the room. 'Light the lamps, Deb, and look you trim them well.'
> She busied herself with mending the fire, trying to coax a flame. The past was a dream, and lost to her. She could not live there now.

For practical reasons, the above is a very short flashback, but within that framework the first paragraph could be extended to cover the whole of the love affair alluded to, with the narration spread over several pages.

In fact, if you are going to use a flashback at all, it is probably best to make it a substantial one, thereby minimising the chance of confusion. Some very successful historicals have consisted of one long flashback, framed by the first and last chapters, notably *Immortal Queen* by Elizabeth Byrd, which begins and ends with the execution of Mary Stuart.

Choreography

An odd word? Not really, since there are writers who find problems in deciding how to move their characters not only through time but through space, not in the context of science fiction (which is dealt with by another author in this series) but simply in terms of moving them about a room.

You may have heard somewhere that such and such a percentage of dialogue must be broken up by a certain amount of action, and vice versa. Don't let it worry you.

It can certainly be useful to use a small action such as 'he set down the tankard' or 'she stared out between the mullions' to indicate who is speaking during a substantial piece of dialogue without recourse to an intrusive use of names; but as far as proportion is concerned you will do better to let the vision in your mind dictate it.

The important thing is to have sufficient going on (if you are writing prose) to sustain the picture in the reader's imagination, without self-consciously interposing action merely because you think it is time you did. A golden rule is: when you have nothing to say, don't say it.

Remember that everything on every page should carry the story forward, and try to avoid static situations with everyone busily milling about but not going anywhere – a sort of frenetic Morris dance that never moves off the spot.

It is not always easy to see where the dramatic peaks in your story should come; neither is it easy or even possible for anyone else to lay down a formula which will suit every case.

In a stage play, the run-up to a crisis will be needed at the curtain of each act; otherwise a fickle audience may decide to stay in the bar after the interval instead of returning to the seats. A sad occurrence, but not unknown, particularly in the case of jaded critics who have come only because they are obliged to.

A short story will require only one situation, one climax; the situation with which it opened will be resolved in one way or another at the end, while a long book with several sub-plots will probably take us through many more than three before the final resolution.

We will explore the dramatic content, and how to make the most of it, in the next section.

9
Bringing it
to Life

If variety is the spice of life, drama is the life-blood of fiction. Every story needs an element of drama, to keep our interest alive, to heighten the suspense, and to involve its readers in the destinies of the characters. Without it, we are left with a mere account, a list of facts that nobody wants to read; and in a tough market the work, however meticulous, will stand a very slim chance of publication.

With historicals it is particularly tempting, as we have seen, to relax and let the setting take the strain, imagining that achieving publication is something like sitting an exam: put in all the right things, observe the rules, gain sufficient marks for accuracy and presto! We have passed, and success is assured. Alas, this is not so. There is no set criterion, labelled 'publication standard', at which a writer can aim with any degree of confidence, although there may well be a standard below which he dare not fall.

Since publishers and agents are in business for business reasons, they are under no divine obligation to see our work into print; indeed, if they accepted everything that passed through their hands they would soon be out of business altogether. In creating a work of fiction we are offering something dependent on the whim of the beholder. A novel is essentially non-essential; unlike food or clothing in that no one is compelled to have it, since everyone can live perfectly well without it. What, then, is the answer?

Quite simply, what we have to do is make the publishers an offer they can't refuse. This means writing something that excites, that so catches the imagination as to convince a prospective buyer that this is something he cannot afford to miss.

While there is no golden recipe for such a work, there are three factors which can be relied upon to militate in your favour: an original idea, a crisp and individual writing style, and the skilful management of dramatic content.

An original idea you must find for yourself; sometimes it may come to you through the inversion of a cliché situation.

A good writing style will develop naturally or not at all. It arises largely from the way in which you see things yourself; if a witty or amusing observation comes to you on some point of the story, don't be afraid to use it – only be careful not to state it as coming from yourself (author talking) in the narrative, but to put it into the mouth or mind of one of your characters.

The third is something you can consciously acquire.

Bringing out the drama

In contemplating the likely course of the plot you will be able to pinpoint several key events on which the story hinges; these are the scenes you will want, and need, to highlight. Cinematically speaking, while some stretches of the action are viewed in 'long shot' to encompass a broad canvas, these crucial scenes will need to be seen in close-up to have their full value. You will want to impress them on the reader's mind, to isolate them in sharp detail in order to give them sufficient weight, and to show their significance in the light of what follows. To do this you must be prepared to study the art of contrast.

'Negative' space

If you look at a famous portrait, or a brilliant photograph, or the lighting of a stage set while a leading character is making an important speech, you will notice one thing: the light, and therefore the attention, is focused in one place only. The rest is in shadow, in soft focus, or merely suggested in subdued, inconspicuous shades.

To do this without benefit of paintbrush, camera or lights may seem less easy, but it can be done. The technique lies in separating scenes of high drama, conflict or deep emotion between spells of comparative tranquillity, so that there are light and shade in your picture, strong images in the foreground, contrasting sharply with the 'negative space' of the background to give them emphasis. As any artist will know, if the negative spaces, meaning the gaps or intervals between the 'positive' forms, are wrong, the forms themselves cannot be right either.

This theory is well understood in the East; the Chinese speak of the Yin-Yang principle, which means the interplay of the positive with the negative to achieve the natural balance of the whole. If you intersperse your dramatic scenes with more peaceful passages, not only will you successfully highlight the key points of your story, but we as readers will have a chance to catch our breath, and be all the more ready and willing to hold it again as the next crisis looms on the horizon, ideally at the close of the chapter.

Think for a moment of the comic who raps out joke after joke without a breathing space; for five minutes he is hilarious. After ten his humour begins to pall on us . . . it takes little imagination to know how we would feel if he kept it up for an hour or more. Everything needs variety, a space in which to catch up with ourselves; any story that remains on the same level all the way through, whether it be high or low, ceases to be an entertainment and becomes an endurance test. Tragedy is the more effective when juxtaposed with comedy, and vice versa. They need both light and shade to give them form.

Having spaced our crucial scenes, how to enhance them?

Pacing the action

If they are action scenes, e.g. a battle, a fight to the death, a moment of peril in the physical sense, the pace and tension can be increased by shortening sentences to give the impression of speed, of urgency and anxiety. Avoid using long complicated phrases, or atmosphere will suffer. Keep moving at all costs, even the cost of grammatical construction, since in a moment of danger nouns and even verbs may be dispensed with in the interests of tension. Keep the adrenalin flowing; save your more leisurely, contemplative observations for another time.

If, on the other hand, the occasion is an emotional one, the opposite will apply. The scene may be described at a much slower pace, but in sharp detail, every moment being savoured.

The 'frozen moment'

In the Kabuki theatre of Japan, a technique is used, at a crucial point such as a murder, of 'freezing' the action totally in a momentary tableau of stillness. This, in the midst of rapid though formalised activity, has the effect of impressing the picture on the spectator as something to be remembered.

This device can also be utilised in writing, by stopping the action for a moment while going into the mind of one of the characters. There is a moment in an emotional crisis when the mind recoils from what is presented, and runs away to the refuge of everyday things. In a vain attempt to blot out the inescapable, it imprints itself with whatever the individual is looking at, or touching, or even is able to smell. In describing this, you can capture something of a character's heightened senses during a moment of trauma.

You will also find that you now have the perfect 'trigger' for either a reverie or a flashback, should one be needed later on, as the sight of that same object or place will inevitably recall the scene to the character, regardless of the passage of time. Even the scent of a remembered flower can be painfully, irresistibly nostalgic – but if you name a flower, be sure it is one that could have been growing at the time!

Flowery language

Finally, a caution against over-writing, the tendency to go over the top into absurdity and worse. This is an ever-present hazard to the writer of historical fiction, which lends itself so readily to sugary sentimentality or flamboyant over-description in the style of the earlier – and not very good – Hollywood production. Whatever you have to tell us will come over best in clean, economical language; the starker the statement, the stronger the impact.

Select the words you use with loving care; the right noun needs no adjective, just as the right verb needs no adverb to qualify it. The hallmark of good writing is the one word that dispenses with the need for many.

10
Getting it Right

So you thought you'd finished? I've got news for you. Some of the most serious work is about to begin. You have planned it, got it all on paper — what more is there to do?

The answer is that now you have spun the raw yarn into fabric you are about to make up the garment, cutting, stitching, fitting and pressing until you have a perfect 'fit'; there must be no seam crooked, no stitches showing.

Don't be put off by this prospect; it is arguably the most rewarding part of the process of writing. You will be surprised when you turn back to the beginning to find how much you can improve on what you have done, especially if, ideally, you have had the time and forbearance to put it away for a month or so before embarking on this stage. Once immersed in revision you will be aware of a growing excitement, and if you have done your job well, will find yourself tempted to read on from page to page in forgetfulness of what you are meant to be doing!

Think of this stage as a kind of literary grooming, the clearing away of extraneous matter. You owe it to yourself, for all the work and loving — or hating! — care you have put into it so far, to give your novel its best possible chance, to turn it out looking not just good, but professional.

Put your heart into the work and enjoy it. This, incidentally, is the point at which you will find exactly what is needed for that earlier chapter (the opening?) that eluded you so maddeningly at the time.

Start at the beginning and go through the whole thing methodically (I did this no less than four times on my first historical), then you will know that nothing has been missed. Not that the finished volume will ever quite match up to your first vision: even after several drafts, editing and proof reading, you may still kick yourself when you see it in print on account of that one word you are now convinced would have been better!

Forget about the counsel of perfection and do the best job you can. The following are among the things you will be looking for.

Repetition

Repetition may take the form of duplicated information. For example, if you have told us in dialogue that someone is expected to arrive on the stage coach, it is not necessary also to show him arriving, unless the actual event is to deviate from the expectation. If it doesn't, you have wasted words in telling us the same thing twice.

Other forms of repetition to look out for are making the same point at two different junctures of the story, and the too frequent use of a favourite word which you may not even have recognised as a favourite. When you do, it will stick out like a sore thumb!

Empty dialogue

By this is meant dialogue that is little more than idle conversation and which fulfils none of the requirements outlined in the section on dialogue: providing information, defining character and carrying the story further.

Variations from recorded history

This cannot be excused. If the story and the known facts are at variance, it is, sadly, your story that will have to give way. Readers of historical fiction are often quite knowledgeable, and there will inevitably be someone somewhere who will delight in putting you right. If your editor is the one to catch you out, your work may not even get as far as publication, and certainly not without radical and problematic rewriting.

Idle words

These, by definition, are words that are not working for you. They include those which say, not precisely what you want them to, but somewhere near it. Ask yourself whether 'near enough is good enough'; if it isn't, root them out and replace them with better ones. Don't use tired old words any more than you would use tired old clichés; they are simply so much luggage for your story to carry. Some writers, usually journalists for whom every word must necessarily do the work of three, will tell you to cut out all adjectives and adverbs. I don't personally subscribe to this, as the judicious use of one or the other in an unusual combination can be extremely effective; but make sure you don't put them in out of habit, e.g. *'nice* cup of tea' or 'a *pretty* girl', or that old cliché *'sparkling* eyes'. There are much better words you can use to tell us something really interesting.

It is at this stage, when you have the whole story before you, that you can really see what is needed and what should be pruned away.

By pruned, I mean the sort of editing that is known as 'tightening', i.e. the removal of redundant words, sentence by sentence. Here is an example:

'While she ran between the trees down the road towards the park, she could tell that the dog was excited, because he was barking and making a great deal of noise!'

This could be tightened effectively to:

'Running down the tree-lined road to the park, she sensed the dog's excitement from his noisy barking.'

You will have shortened the sentence from 30 words to 17, without losing anything of the meaning. This kind of treatment can be used to advantage when you can see that the story is too long for its weight, and you will be surprised to see how easily you can reduce it by a couple of thousand words if you have a lot of 'loose writing' such as in the first example. Moreover, you will probably find that the finished draft is an improvement on the first, not only because it is shorter but because it has gained more impact and better pace. I use the word 'pruning' for this process advisedly. Writing is like roses: the harder you prune it, the better it blooms.

If, however, you have been advised to cut a long story in length by a quarter or more which, sadly, is not all that unusual, you will have to use more drastic measures, since no amount of tightening is going to remove a quarter of its length.

The only way to do this is as if you were clearing a drawer, turning the whole thing upside down on the bed, emptying everything out. Then forget about looking for something to throw away, but look instead for what you can't do without. You will find that you have put back what you really need, and can throw the rest unlamented into the dustbin.

Don't succumb to the temptation to look at the rejects and sorrow over them. If you feel they are too good to throw away, put them unseen into a file and save them for another day.

Nothing is wasted, and you are now aiming your sights towards success.

Sententiousness

This is just a fancy word for moralising, for passing judgement on an incident or a character, and it is something you must never do, no matter how strongly you feel. If your story has sprung from anger against injustice or cruelty – fine. It will have come out in the writing without your having to point it out. Present us with the facts and leave us to reach our own conclusions. Nothing is less attractive to the reader than an author who is continually climbing on to his soapbox and holding forth.

Irrelevant research

Resist the temptation to leave in those little oddments that enchanted you in the process of research unless they are truly relevant to the story. We have already talked about this, so only a reminder is needed here.

But another aspect comes to mind in that while you were writing the first draft, you may wisely have put in a number of dates and/or references to your characters' ages at certain points to keep you on the right lines as the plot developed. Now is the time for you to go back and take out about 90 per cent of them, leaving only what is needed by the reader. The house is built now: you can remove the scaffolding without fear of it falling down.

Over-writing

We have already said something about over-writing in an earlier section, but a few more words will not come amiss. Flowery writing, mentioned earlier, is one example. You know it when you see it; it includes writing about the Victorians in the sugary terms of their own Valentines and Christmas cards, or lacing the narrative with an artificial primness. Leave such sentimentality and prudery for the dialogue where it belongs. On no account indulge in it yourself.

It is also a great temptation when writing about an earlier age, a time perhaps of great artistic achievement such as the Renaissance, to make a conscious attempt to write what we will call 'great literature': don't try. A natural and honest style is far more appealing than any attempt to ape the writing styles of classical authors. Their modes of expression cannot, in any case, be reproduced by you or anyone else, having come to them naturally and simply, as will your own. Dr Johnson spoke the definitive words on this: 'Read over your compositions, and wherever you meet with a passage which you think is particularly fine, strike it out.' Harsh words, perhaps; but the truth is often painful.

In this connection it is worth bearing in mind that the great Jane Austen and Charles Dickens were not writing historicals; their novels were contemporary, as they were writing of their own time. Dickens in particular has a great lesson for us all: his characterisation was superb (if a little larger than life) in that every single individual was presented as a whole, living and breathing personality from the central characters right down to the coachman or the clerk of the court at a trial. Read these authors, learn from them, but remember not to take them as models for the historical; that is not what they wrote.

Negligence

Whether this shows in sloppy research or in any other aspect of your work, be assured that show it will. Enough said.

If you read down the initial letters of these headings, you will see that they spell 'REVISION'; a little mnemonic to help you as a checklist. You will also have noticed that they all have a negative connection: they all refer to something to be taken out, and this is, of course, an important aspect of revision, which is the author's own means of editing.

But there is also a positive aspect of revision which you cannot afford to ignore. This is the opportunity to stand back and look at your work as a whole, to see where there is a dull passage crying out to be refreshed, a missed opportunity for a valuable scene in something important you have only mentioned in passing, or even something as seemingly trivial as two names sufficiently alike for the reader to have to make a conscious effort to distinguish them. Now is the time to go through your manuscript in detail, combing out the dead hair and brushing and polishing what remains to the brightest possible shine. In today's competitive market, your story will need all the help you can give it.

Length

It may be that your revision reveals something as drastic as that you have written three or four times as much as any publisher is likely to take – or equally, not nearly enough to constitute a usable manuscript. In the case of its being far too long, you must look out for:

Loose writing of the sort that takes fifteen words to do the work of three, two pages to achieve the action of two paragraphs.

Unnecessary sub-plots which merely divert the reader's attention away from the main theme (you may find that you have material for two other books in there; be brave, cut it out and save it for another story).

The temptation to put in everything that might possibly have happened along the way, a trap into which many of us fall with our first long work.

For all our fears that we could 'never write enough words to fill a book' (and the majority of historical fiction does fall into the novel category), it is very unlikely that, having once started and got into your stride, you will find that you haven't written enough. But if it should be the case, don't attempt to lengthen it by 'padding'. You will simply find yourself putting back all those passages of inferior quality you took out because you knew they were not working for you. This sort of contrivance always shows, and you would do far better to start again, expressing your story in one of the shorter forms, perhaps a play for radio, or even a short story. The probable explanation is that the original idea related to an incident rather than to a long sequence of events, and was not suitable material for a novel of any length. If you are still convinced that it *wants* (a word carefully chosen here) to be a novel, you will need to develop the lives and qualities of its characters with an expertise you are unlikely to have at your fingertips when writing a first book.

Be wise; put the typescript away while you write something else and then go back to it with a fresh eye. In the writing of the second book, you will have acquired more of your craft and be better fitted to tackle the problems of the first. We learn something from everything we write, even if it is only letters to friends, and none of it is wasted or forgotten.

So what is the 'right' length for a historical? Good question! It has caused a good deal of nail biting in its time, for the simple reason that there is no one answer. It depends on the requirements of the publisher, the state of play between him and the printers, the costs of production, the type of story, and not least, *the demands of the story*. This last and your own exacting standards are likely to be your best guide in the matter.

If the editor to whom you offer it really likes it — 'loves it', as they say in the trade — is prepared to 'godmother' it and see it through to the editorial board, but knows they couldn't use it at its present length, you can be asked to shorten it (most likely) or lengthen it (which is rarely the case), and it will then be up to you to decide if the game is worth the candle. In this case, consider carefully whether your hurt pride really warrants turning down the chance of publication. Remember that the publisher has one great advantage that you lack: experience. Make no snap decisions; think it over calmly, so that you can reach a balanced judgement (bearing in mind that the customer is always right)

Another factor is likely to influence the requirement of length, and that is category. But before we go into that in the next chapter, a few important words.

Presentation

You probably already know that your work should be typed, in double spacing (to give editors and printers room for their instructions between the lines), and on one side only of 8½ x 11 paper opaque enough not to show through. It also needs good margins. Publishers vary in their requirements as to whether or not you should fasten the pages together, but on one point they are universal: don't use paper clips or pins. The latter are lethal, while the former have an infuriating tendency to pick up other material from the desk.

For my first submission I carefully stapled the typescript into chapters, thinking it would be easier to handle at the other end. I quickly learned wisdom on finding out that some unfortunate person had had to ruin her fingernails taking them all out again before the typescript could be dealt with. The best thing, I was told, is to number the pages carefully and leave them separate, packing them for posting in a stationery box or a large jiffy bag.

Editors and publishers' readers apparently prefer to take one page at a time, read it and turn it face down on another pile, rather than have to wrestle with a large unwieldy bundle, especially as a good deal of reading is done at home on the knee.

You owe it to yourself to take this amount of care in presentation. Call it showmanship, if you like, but it is worthwhile. Think of an editor as a human being; she (it is usually 'she') comes in on a Monday morning after a good weekend, or maybe a bad one spent plodding through someone else's unreadable work, to find yet another stack of typescripts lying in ambush on her desk. There may be as many as twenty piling up, many of which will be at best incompetent and at worst a waste of time. Some are handwritten, some typed with a ribbon so old as to be almost indecipherable – I even heard of one sent in handwritten on a roll of shelf paper! – some on paper so thin that page 2 shows through while she is trying to read page 1, and maybe even one running into three or four fat bundles, usually a boring biography of someone nobody has heard of or has any wish to know.

And there among them is a clean, well-presented MS with a professional air about it, suggesting that it was sent in by someone who at least knows how to put a book together. Ask yourself, which of these would you be likely to reach for while the other hand fishes in the drawer for the aspirins?

Such a submission shines from the 'slush pile' like a daffodil on a dungheap. This is not to say that the others on the pile will not be read at all; in a conscientious office everything will be looked at, if only by an outside reader for a first screening. But the sad truth is that the slush pile is the publishers' name for the growing heap of unsolicited manuscripts on which yours is likely to alight, and it must be faced that the epithet is often justified.

Submitting your MS

Should you write an accompanying letter? If you do, keep it brief. Simply say that you are offering the book for consideration, state the theme briefly if you wish, mention the title, and enclose adequate postage and a self-addressed label for its return.

I myself don't think there is any advantage to be gained by writing to a publisher asking if he is interested before submitting the MS. Publishers are busy people already flooded with unwanted material, and the easiest and most likely answer is No.

If your MS is returned to you, send it out again. But don't send it out looking dog-eared, thereby advertising that it has already been turned down by someone else. Type a new title page (which will state the title, approximate length in words, your pen name if you use one, and your real name and postal address), and a new final page (which should also bear your name and address), and if the intermediate pages are crumpled, a warm iron should do the rest.

If all this sounds to you like an unnecessary fuss over details, think of it like this. You wouldn't send your child to that important first job interview in a grubby shirt and scuffed shoes so don't you owe the same consideration to this, your first brain-child? As the saying goes, you know it makes sense.

One thing that cannot be stressed too heavily is *never send out anything of which you haven't kept a copy*. Horror stories abound of MSS mislaid or destroyed, lost in the post or accidentally burned. And don't, as someone of my acquaintance once did, send off a batch of rough notes, thinking that the actual work would be done by 'someone in the office'. Not only was it not — why should anyone else be expected to do our donkeywork? — but his notes vanished without trace, consigned, no doubt, to the w.p.b.

No, of course he hadn't kept a copy.

And that's a pity. It was a damned good story he had to tell.

11
The Prospect
Before Us

There has long been a myth that first novels never get published. This is demonstrably untrue, as the long list of 'firsts' which became world-wide bestsellers shows.

What is undeniably true is that for a first novel to be published it must in some way be outstanding, since it must make its way through formidable barriers. No first novel has ever made its mark by being just as good as somebody else's: it has to be better. It also has to be seen by the right person at the right time, and this is where an element of luck comes in. We have all been depressed by the sight of bookshelves full of work which is no better, in our own opinion perhaps much worse, than that which we have just had turned down. Where is the justice, we may ask ourselves? I sent my MS to the same publisher and got it back with a rejection slip.

Reasons for rejection

The possible reasons for rejection are many, and may have little to do with the quality of your work. Publishers, like others, are largely in the hands of accountants, and their judgement has of necessity to be influenced as much by predictable sales as by merit. And the book you felt to be inferior to yours may simply have been more commercial. It may have commanded a fat subsidy from the sale of American rights, a factor which many publishers are taking more and more into consideration. Or it may merely have fallen into a more saleable category within the genre.

Yours, given for the moment that it is equally well written, may have a less wide appeal by reason of its subject matter, or its period; some periods are virtually 'written out', with the result that it becomes more and more difficult to market anything of that era. There may be a current trend for a particular type of story, say the family saga, the so-called bodice-ripper or 'hot historical', or the 250,000-word blockbuster, and your story doesn't fall into any of these categories. If so, you may be luckier when the trend has changed.

You will, if you are wise, be well on with the next book by the time the blow falls: turn the MS around, send it out somewhere else and concentrate on the work in hand. The new book will be better, it is bound to be; and you will at least have another iron in the fire. Never sit wringing your hands over the fate of something you have just sent out; it may be months or years before it finds a home and in the meantime precious time's a-wasting.

At a recent conference, author William Horwood encouraged his audience of aspiring writers with these words: 'Be proud of your achievement whether published or not, and don't let your nearest and dearest belittle it. Persistence pays more than talent.'

Creative-writing student Peter Cross expressed the same idea in a haiku:

> He who tries in vain
> Should not be called a failure:
> Hold him in esteem.

Workshops and writers' groups

Success will come, in time, if you want it enough. Enough, that is, to put the same amount of energy and dedication into launching yourself as a writer as you would into starting any other career. Success comes to those with the right combination of talent and a professional attitude. You may find it helpful and supportive during this period to belong to a writers' circle or other workshop in your area. The advantages of such groups are numerous, not least being the contact with others who share your problems, triumphs and disappointments and can not only keep you in touch with marketing and publishing news but provide a yardstick by which to measure your own progress. But perhaps most valuable of all is the exchange of constructive criticism in the right spirit. So what do we mean by the right spirit?

The giving and taking of criticism

There are two ways in which to take criticism. We can take it like prima donnas, convinced that whatever we have written is so perfect that it cannot possibly be improved; or we can take it like professionals, examine and consider it, asking ourselves whether, since it has come from a reader (the audience at whom our work is aimed), there may not be some truth in it from which to benefit.

There are also two ways in which to offer it. There is the destructive criticism which says merely 'No, that's wrong' or 'It bored me, I never read that sort of thing', without offering any practical suggestions as to improvement. This sort of remark stems from either a misplaced sense of superiority or indifference to a fellow member's work, and in either case should be firmly discouraged.

The constructive critic will listen for things that could be improved, and never indulge in a mere 'put-down' for its own sake. The last thing a fledgling writer needs is discouragement.

Always remember when offering advice that you are levelling criticism at someone else's child. For this reason, in a well-run group, no one member will be permitted to criticise indefinitely without reading aloud something of his own, if only to keep him or her in touch with how it feels to be on the receiving end.

Don't be afraid to join a circle, or think you are not 'good enough' because you are not yet published. Many people join as unpublished hopefuls and go on to success, not a little of which may be attributable to their membership of the group. And this brings me to another point: please don't abandon the circle when you achieve publication. You will have gained from it in ways you may not recognise; stay on, and try to give some of that help back to the newcomers.

Categories within the genre

How much difference is there between the various types of historical? Let us consider for a moment, for each has its own characteristics with particular appeal to different sectors of publishing. If, for instance, you were to offer a typical Harlequin romance to Viking or Houghton Mifflin or vice versa, you would be courting rejection which would have little to do with the merit of your work.

We will take them one at a time.

The historical romance This is the story in which the romantic theme is paramount. The relationship between the man and the woman being all-important, it is less concerned with history for its own sake and will require less in-depth research, although what you do put in must be no less accurate for being relegated to the background. Mills & Boon, the great romantics of the publishing world, have their own successful historical 'list', and if you are aiming at this you will be wise to apply to them for their guidelines. Don't be deceived, there is more to writing 'formula' fiction than meets the eye, and many an experienced writer has barked her shins on their illustrious — and very lucrative — doorstep!

There are other houses which take historical romances, and each will have its own requirements as to length, the degree of 'steam' — sex scenes — and how explicit they like these to be. The main characters for the romance will be limited to three or four; the viewpoint will almost inevitably be the woman's, who will need to be present on every page and you will therefore have made sure that she is interesting enough in her own right to sustain her responsibility.

The 'hot historical' or 'bodice-ripper'   Obviously, this is the steamiest of all. Since the commercial success of *Forever Amber*, many writers have jumped on the wagon and have done very well out of it. However, the big wave appears to be receding, so unless writing explicit sex is your forte – and if it is, by all means stick to what you are best at and don't be put off by what Aunt Ermintrude will think – you may be better advised to look elsewhere for your break-through. There are a number of writers already well established in this field and, as the publishing houses dealing in it are limited, you are unlikely to do more than nudge the ranks in the UK. In the USA, however, the outlook is much more promising.

On the practical side, the number of characters holding centre stage is likely to be similar to that of the romance, while the length tends to merge with that of the blockbuster, although there is a definite gap between the lengths of 80,000 to 120,000 words usually required in this category and that of the blockbuster. Apparently publishers find anything in between difficult to cost and price acceptably.

The 'blockbuster' of 250,000 words   This is a major project and not to be undertaken lightly. It demands a broad, spectacular canvas, if exotic so much the better, yet it must avoid being over-written.

In short, this is not what I would recommend to the inexperienced as the best thing with which to begin. But if that is what your story has become and you feel confident that you have done it as well as 'the next guy', go ahead and give it its chance. Who am I to judge your potential as a writer?

On the whole, these enormous novels are best directed at the larger and more commercial publishing houses, who have sufficient money for advertising to give them the necessary 'hype' (hyper-launch) to get them off the ground for the unknown author. And in order to justify this kind of expensive publicity they have got to be good enough to ensure that all the money is not only recouped, but shows a profit.

The big adventure   This may cover the colonisation of a wilderness to create a new nation, the course of a crusade or a revolution, or adventure on a smaller scale such as the pirate sagas of Rafael Sabatini. It will rely heavily on action and excitement, while the romantic interest will be peripheral. This type of fiction has a predominantly male readership, and it is necessary to have a good understanding of what men enjoy reading. This is the group into which James Clavell's *Shogun* falls – if you can call it falling!

A writer should try to cultivate a degree of androgyny, that quality which helps us to see into the minds of both sexes. Successful romances have been written by men hiding behind feminine pseudonyms (interesting that it used to be the other way about!).

The family saga   Sagas have recently been enjoying a wave of popularity which may or may not be on the ebb. But there is no denying that a good one, with characters to whom the reader is reluctant to say goodbye, can be the start of a long and successful career for its author. Ideally a saga needs a background which has not already been over-exploited by other writers and the best and strongest possible characterisation. Once established, the story can continue through volume after volume – each, of course, a separate novel – pursuing the careers of family members down through several generations, each of which will bring a subtle change of period and attitude. For good examples of this genre, see the works of Jean Stubbs, Margaret Thomson Davies and Iris Gower; they have all taken little known backgrounds, brought them to life with flesh and blood human beings, and done very well with them.

There is a definite market for this type of book, as the popularity of Catherine Cookson demonstrates.

The straight historical   This may be defined as a serious, middle-of-the-road novel about the problems of one or more persons who lived in a time remote from our own. Those problems must, for a genuine historical, arise from the time and climate in which they lived. If they do not, it might as well have been written as a contemporary novel, and would in that case be all the better for not appearing contrived and artificial.

The optimum number of characters for this type of story will be much the same as for any other straight novel, i.e. preferably not more than four or five main characters with others on the periphery. The length, however, is usually a little more flexible than for the contemporary, most publishers allowing a further five to ten thousand words over and above the normal 75,000 to 80,000 to accommodate the necessary background research.

If you feel that this is what you have written, and you think you've got it right, go for one of the more up-market publishers who will be likely to appreciate your work.

The nostalgia novel   This covers anything dealing with a period outside the present day but still within living memory. Most novels on the two world wars and their respective aftermaths fall into this group, which has distinct advantages – and disadvantages – in the way of research.

It is only too easy to feel confident that we remember the details of something through which we lived ourselves. And this, believe it or not, is where we are most likely to be wrong. While we may have 100 per cent recall on certain conversations we ourselves held at the time, or even important broadcasts such as the declaration of war in 1939 (and no, it wasn't Winston Churchill), can we be certain that we are right about the exact date of that soft autumnal day ... and was it a Saturday or a Sunday? Well, we do remember that we were digging in the garden ... and the lunch was cooking ... or was it dinner?

There is the problem in a nutshell. The solution is to research the nostalgia period as thoroughly as you would any other time in history, and only embellish with your own recollections when you have verified the accuracy of your facts.

The great advantage is that here we have the assistance of newspaper reports and other archives. The twentieth century is documented in more detail than any other period: make full use of its facilities. Any major library can provide you with any amount of data culled from their vast newspaper archives, and most newspaper offices elsewhere keep back numbers going back some years. If you are lucky enough to have friends with specialised knowledge of early railways and telephone systems, you will find their help invaluable in establishing that genuine feeling of authenticity so sorely needed by this type of novel. An otherwise excellent film about the battle of Britain was marred for me by seeing the heroine take off her WAAF skirt to reveal stretch nylon briefs, an article of clothing unknown in Britain in 1940.

Failure in this aspect is likely to result in someone who remembers it at first hand, and has picked up your work with a feeling of pleasurable anticipation, muttering 'Hmph ... written by some youngster who wasn't there and doesn't know what he's talking about!' and tossing it aside in disappointment.

This does not mean that if you didn't live through the period you shouldn't be writing about it. What it means is that, regardless of your age or generation, you must take more care with research than would seem to be necessary at first glance. If, for example, you set your story in the World War II era, don't forget the blackout restrictions (and when they ended), a matter too often overlooked in TV productions. Make sure about the details of food rationing, its effects on domestic arrangements (e.g. each customer had to 'register' with one shop and couldn't buy anywhere else), the Black Market and the different dates after the official end of hostilities on which the various foodstuffs, clothing, coal and even petrol came 'off the ration'. Remember that petrol was subject to different restrictions according to whether it was for private or commercial use, and that 'commercial' was dyed pink to distinguish it, there being a penalty for any private motorist caught with it in his tank.

Bear in mind details such as the Restriction of Supplies Order, 1941, which limited the quantities of any goods whatever to be offered for sale in the shops, and the fact that for a large part of the war years no one, once established in one part of the UK, was permitted to travel to another sector without a permit from the government.

Familiarise yourself with the times when discotheques and jiving first appeared on the scene; likewise when world air travel was restored, and when its glamorous air hostesses, as they were then called, arrived to supersede the film star as every girl's career ambition. Know when the package holiday took the place of the holiday camp, even when the Mini was launched on the market (1961) to become the universal English runabout car. This last could have tripped me up in *Goodbye, Sally*, had not my sharp-eyed editor picked it up; she reminded me that the Mini was not yet around in the year of which I was writing, and I hastily changed the reference to a Morris Minor. You see how careful we need to be.

There are inevitably too many people about who *know* for you to risk taking chances. It takes only one little slip (or pair of knickers) to ruin the illusion, and as much of the appeal of the nostalgia piece lies in the allure of a sentimental journey into a past only half forgotten, it is particularly important to get it right.

As you can see, it has pitfalls all its own; before you send it anywhere, check absolutely *everything*. The nostalgia novel is as much a historical as any other, and needs to be just as meticulously researched.

The above are the main categories into which your work is likely to fall. You may think it strange that I have left discussion of categories until so late in this book: should I not have set them all out at the beginning, so that you could have tailored your work to fit into one of them?

The reason I didn't is because I don't believe the best work is done in this way, especially if you haven't much experience in the field. You can find yourself worrying too much about 'rules' and too little about other more important aspects.

It is infinitely preferable to write your story first, letting it find its own style and length, and only then consider into which category it falls. Categories are, to my mind, more the business of the publisher than of the author, having more to do with marketing than with creating. Perhaps this is why so few publishers are in the habit of commissioning fiction, feeling that this results in writers trying to cram their work into moulds that don't truly fit.

12
Getting Published

Now that you have finished work on your story (at least for the time being) you are faced with the problem of where to submit it. At this point, the question inevitably arises: should you get an agent?

Let me rephrase that; should you *try* to get an agent?

Literary agents

The truth is that agents, like anyone else, are in the business to make a living, and are unlikely to take you on without some assurance that your work is likely to contribute to it. That assurance will come from the fact that you are already published, or have received a worthwhile acceptance for the work in hand. Even then, the agent you need will be the one who insists on first reading your work — published or not — to satisfy himself that what you are writing is what he can successfully promote on your behalf, i.e. that the markets at which your work is best aimed are those he knows most about.

The answer I usually give to this question is to do your own legwork, get a publisher to accept your work, and then consider looking for an agent. Ignore the prophets of gloom who tell you that you don't stand a chance of publication without an agent, it is simply not true. It is undeniable that publishers tend to look first at the MSS coming in from agencies, since these have already passed a first screening and come with a recommendation other than your own; but it is also true that they are always on the lookout for the outstanding find from the unsolicited pile, whose author is unrepresented and therefore less likely to drive a hard bargain over the contract. They also, being human, are susceptible to the thrill of discovering talent.

So, having got your first acceptance, are you going to need an agent? And if you get one, what will he do for you? There are obvious advantages, in that he will negotiate contracts for you, see to it that they are fair to both sides, and have no deceptive clauses that could militate against you. He can also handle diplomatically any disagreements you may have with the publishing house, saving you the necessity of arguing it out with your editor and possibly souring the relationship.

He will also be in a position to help you place your future work, and it is clearly much easier and less embarrassing for him to say, 'This is terrific stuff, and worth better terms than you are offering' than it would be for you. If, on the other hand, it is not such terrific stuff, he can tell you so in confidence, giving you the chance of improving it before a publisher sees it.

What he should *not* be expected to do is edit your work himself, or spend his own time and money on trying to sell your first efforts, unless he is confident of their success and willing to take a flyer. It costs him money to set up a file for each new client; it is only reasonable for him to expect a fair return on his outlay.

You will, of course, have to pay him, usually about 10% of your earnings on anything he negotiates for you, a little more on foreign sales since he will probably be employing another agent in the country concerned. You may regard this as a disadvantage, although a good agent will help you to earn more than enough to compensate for his fee. A 'bad' one, i.e. the one whose working methods are out of tune with your own and therefore cramp your style, who either drives you too hard or sits back and forgets you altogether, will give you cause for regret, although he or she may be an excellent choice for someone else.

If, having weighed up the pros and cons, you decide that you do need an agent, make sure that you approach the right one for you. The wrong one, as one publisher told me, can be the kiss of death. There is a long list in the back of the *Literary Market Place* giving names and addresses of agents (and also publishers and their requirements), from which you could pick one with a pin without having any idea of how the 'marriage' will work out. A better method is to seek a recommendation from a fellow writer who has an agent he is happy with, bearing in mind that few agents deal with short stories, articles or poetry. Then, having secured your typescript's acceptance, write to or ring up the agent of your choice and ask if he (or she) is willing to act for you.

Don't be offended if you are turned down; there really are too few agents for the number of writers, and while the reply, 'Sorry, my list is full,' may be a kindly euphemism for 'Thanks, but no thanks!' it may also truly mean just what it says.

You will be wise not to be dazzled by the fame of very large firms; it is too easy for your little-known work to be overlooked while the agents take care of the Jeffrey Archers and Barbara Cartlands, the lucrative clients from whom the big money comes. You will do better with a smaller agency which prefers to stay small and give individual attention to all its clients.

Having said all this, it is only fair to you to add that television plays are notoriously difficult to place if unsolicited, i.e. neither commissioned nor submitted by an agent. If this is what you are writing, you may not get far without an agent.

Writers' associations

If you don't want an agent, or even if you do, you can only benefit by joining the Authors' Guild of America, who will vet contracts for you, give you valuable advice and keep you in touch with publishing news.

The Writers' Guild of America is also excellent, although perhaps more closely concerned with writers for TV and radio; and as the two societies work together in matters of policy, you stand to get the benefits of both.

Asking for a decision

So now, with or without the services of an agent, your work has been submitted. You will have to wait many weeks – possibly many months – for a verdict, during which time, if you are wise, you will have started on something new. How long should you wait before enquiring, politely, if a decision has been reached yet?

This varies from publisher to publisher, but if, as you should, you receive an acknowledgement soon after sending it in, allow at least two months and possibly more, before you ask about it. The easiest and quickest answer for them to give if pressed is No. If, however, your work has been kept for six months or longer, it is quite reasonable for you to want an answer, even if it does turn out to be negative, in which case you will at least be free to offer it elsewhere. I do know of one case where a publisher held on to a MS for many months without the hapless author hearing any news, after which they did decide to publish; but this is definitely not the norm.

Let us now assume that your work has been accepted. You may be surprised that there is still more work to do! Some time after the congratulations and the euphoria have died away, the champagne cork has been stored among your souvenirs and the cheque you sent for return postage has been returned to you and mounted in the album you've reserved in the hope of press reviews, you will most likely be asked to go and see the editor to discuss possible changes to the script.

Editorial changes

Whatever these changes amount to, try to accept them with a good grace; be thankful that your editor is not the sort to go ahead and make them without consulting you but has given you the opportunity of doing them yourself and in your own way. They may be miniscule – a query on the meaning of a word you have used, a checking of some hiccup in the chronology, the confirmation of some detail of research – or they may involve something quite radical, such as the changing of a main character or a drastic alteration to the plot.

Any proposed changes 'should not alter the author's meaning or intention' (words taken from a publisher's standard form of contract). If they do, or if your story is going to be really carved up, you should consider whether perhaps you have offered your work to the wrong publisher. It is not impossible that all he is interested in is the shell of your story, and wants to use it for something entirely alien to your theme.

Don't panic! Until your signature is on the contract, you are free to withdraw and offer the book elsewhere. And in any case, most reputable publishers of historicals would not dream of such a practice: the point is only raised here to underline the importance of selecting the right one in the first place. And we have already gone into that.

We will assume that all is well, that you have agreed on any changes, done the final revision, and seen your work sent off to the printers. At some point still further into the future, probably many months later when you are fully steeped in the next book, you will find your firstborn once again on your doorstep, demanding to be proof-read (sounds a bit like a real family?).

At this stage, it will have gone through the hands of the copy editor; if she has done her job well, all you will notice is how much better it looks now it is in print. Punctuation, spelling mistakes (try to ensure that there aren't any) and typing errors will have been cleaned up, italics put in where you have indicated by underlining, paragraphing corrected and title pages added, the whole thing smartened up and paginated to appear just as it will between the covers. At last, it looks like a real book. Why are you being asked to read it, yet again?

Proof-reading

You are not expected to pick up 'literals' (printer's errors), although you will be well advised to do so if you notice them, two or three heads being that much better than one. In one of my historicals, where I had proudly put a piece of authentic slang into the mouth of an older man teasing a younger one about his first conquest, as: 'You youngsters start spurring before you can ride,' it was typeset, alas! as 'You youngsters starts *purring. . . .'* And it did come out that way in the published book, having escaped not only my notice but that of several editors along the way! I don't know whether it was a printer's error or if someone else in the chain, failing to recognise the meaning, had altered it with all good intentions to total nonsense. This is a special hazard to writers of historicals, so be warned!

Don't quibble if your double quotes have been changed to single, as this also is a matter of house policy, as is the practice of bringing into line any alternative forms of spelling, such as changing all 'ise' endings to read 'ize', or vice versa, or splitting words like 'someone' or 'onto' into two words – or vice versa! If you argue over trifles you will get nowhere, and will earn yourself the label of Difficult Author.

What you can and should do is read through your work with the fresh eye of many months' hindsight, to see if there is a word here and there for which you have thought of a much better one, if there is a word repeated which now shows up in juxtaposition as too obviously close to its first use, or if you need to change the order of words in a sentence to clarify the meaning.

But bear in mind that if you get too carried away with the improvements at proof stage they are going to cost money, and it may well be your money as you may be asked to pay for them. So go easy, and on no account ask for any alteration that will upset the typesetting by adding to or subtracting from the number of words on the page. If you do, you may find either that your request is ignored or that you are presented with a bill for re-setting the whole chapter to the end.

As always, prevention is easier than cure, and the way to avoid this predicament is to perfect the text as nearly as possible *before* it goes to print.

Do your best to return the corrected proofs (there is a useful section on how to mark them in the *Chicago Manual of Style*) by the date asked for. It may seem to you unreasonable that the publisher wants them back in ten days to a fortnight when he has already had your MS for many months, but you must remember that yours is not the only book he is dealing with; each has to take its turn in going through the system, and a hold-up at your end can make things difficult or even delay publication.

Vanity publishing

There is only one type of publisher who will print exactly what you ask for without any form of editing or correction, and that is the vanity publisher. He can, of course, afford to do this becaue *you* are paying *him*. He is charging you a great deal of money for printing, binding, paper and handling, for which you can expect — what, exactly?

You can certainly expect a volume of sorts, cheaply jacketed and, if your work is a short piece, most likely sandwiched in between other people's work which may be very inferior to yours, because such companies set no standards for acceptance other than an author's willingness to part with money.

Copies will come to you in whatever numbers you have ordered, and these you will be free to sell yourself. Indeed, you will have no choice but to sell them yourself, since these publishers have no outlets through booksellers, the only advertising they do is to attract clients (you!), their publications are never reviewed, and they do not in fact undertake the distribution. The chances are that you will end up with a vast pile of unsaleable books, and a publisher who is laughing all the way to the bank.

Self-publishing

While vanity publishing should be avoided at all costs, it is not to be confused with private or 'desk-top' publishing, which you do on your own behalf, and in which some poets and others engaged in work for unprofitable markets occasionally indulge; once in a rare while it leads on to success. In this, they are not giving anyone else a fat profit for satisfying their vanity but are publishing off their own bat and at their own expense; it is up to you whether you feel it would be worthwhile in your case. Maybe you really have produced something which, although brilliant in its way, had been turned down by publisher after publisher with genuine regret and the explanation that it is simply 'not commercial'; perhaps it is a family history which, although fascinating to those involved, has little appeal to anyone outside the circle. You want it in print for your descendants, to have copies you can pass on to relatives. With a suitable home computer you can turn out a very creditable text, but remember that you will still have to buy both the machine — not cheap — and the paper, and also pay to have the pages bound and put into some form of covers.

Go ahead if you are desperate, but beware of starting such a project without thoroughly costing it out, and don't tell yourself that the local bookshops will sell it for you: they almost certainly won't.

On balance, it is not what I would recommend; even this type of self-publishing can turn out to be much more costly than you think. It is unlikely to make you famous and it definitely won't make you rich.

13
Success and After

Well, you've made it! Your story is finished, published, and enjoying a modest success. You are a published author, perhaps even with a prize under your belt. You have celebrated with friends, signed their copies with pride, saved the champagne cork and mounted your press cuttings in the album, and may quite possibly have been invited to write a sequel. From now on, it is going to be easy ... isn't it? Of course it is.

You sit down at your typewriter or install yourself comfortably with pen and pad in the locked bathroom/garden shed/disused caravan or whichever bizarre spot in the house best attracted the muse when you were struggling with your first one, and your mind is suddenly a total blank.

What has happened to you?

Perhaps it is just a bad day. After all, you've planned it, thought out the characters, done all you should do, learned more about your craft from the writing of the first; why, then are you of all people afflicted with writer's block?

Now, follow that!

The truth is that doubts have begun to creep in. Logic tells you that you can do it, but fear of comparison is holding you back; fear that your next work will somehow fail to measure up to the first, particularly if you have been fortunate enough to start with a big splash. To start your career in this way can be a mixed blessing, heightening as it does the expectations of others, since everything you subsequently produce will be expected to be not merely as good as but better than that spectacular first success. I remember once appealing to my editor that I couldn't be expected to write a prizewinner every time; she smiled and said calmly, 'Well, it was you who set yourself that very high standard.'

Which, flattering as it was, offered me very little for my comfort! Since then I have spoken to so many other authors sharing the same feeling that I have christened it the 'follow-that!' blues.

While you are wrestling to overcome this inhibiting state of mind you find that every time someone says to you 'I did enjoy your first book!' you tend, after the initial thrill, to be filled with new misgivings in case they are disappointed in the next.

Susan Kay, who scooped both the Georgette Heyer and the Betty Trask awards with her first novel *Legacy*, says this: 'My instinct is to run a mile from anyone who kindly inquires when they can expect to see "the next one" on the shelves.' She is by no means alone.

Take heart. This is where that streak of bloody-mindedness that saw you through the first will come to your rescue. You will hear yourself thinking, maybe it was just a flash in the pan – so what? I enjoy writing and I don't care – and so on, until sooner or later the enthusiasm and the excitement of the next idea take over. You grab a pencil thinking, I'll just get that bit down, I can sort it out later if it doesn't work, and after a few false starts you find that you are away, up and running. What is more, the results will be far better than if you had gone on in euphoric overconfidence, believing you had nothing left to learn. We all have something new to learn; the process goes on from the cradle to the grave.

The sorrows of sequels

Sequels are notoriously difficult. While it is very pleasing to be asked to do one, underlining as it does appreciation of the original, the request can put you in a dilemma. For one thing, you have probably said all you had to say on that particular subject, used up your full head of steam and have little more to add, certainly not enough to sustain another full-blown novel. For another, you may quite possibly have killed off one or more of the main characters, and even if you haven't, if all has ended in smiles, there is not a lot of mileage in exploring the happily-ever-after bit, which is likely to be short on drama and essential conflict.

Sequels which match up to or excel their originals are few and far between. But if you are committed to writing one, be advised: don't rush into it straight away, but play for time and leave it until you have another, and preferably different, strong storyline for your characters to play out. Make sure it is an exciting encore, not merely a reprise. If you do this, you will have avoided the trap of flogging a dead horse through a couple of hundred pages.

The third problem with writing a sequel is that you are writing for two distinct readerships: those who have read the first, and those who haven't. Those who have will want a continuing flavour of the first, and will be bored if they have to sit through pages of scene setting and background fill-in for the benefit of those who haven't. These last will have different expectations again, and you will therefore have the added responsibility of producing a story which will stand on its own, the enjoyment of which must not depend on the reader having first read its predecessor.

There is one more point to be taken into consideration, and it is less obvious than the other two. If the sequel has been commissioned by your publisher the probability is that he or she will have a vision of what the book is to be. It is by no means certain that this vision will be matched by yours, and if it doesn't. . . .

On the whole, you may be wise to write your sequel close to the chest, to your own design, and then submit it on spec without offering or discussing it first.

Having sorted out the foregoing difficulties, you are still left with the problem of deciding whose story it is to be. If you have said all you had to say about the main characters and their problems in the first, you are unlikely to be sufficiently fired by their situation in the second, and if you have killed them off at the end, you obviously can't take them any further. There is no way you can use them in a sequel unless you are prepared to make it a 'prequel', which can be even more difficult, since you are unable to keep your options open.

You may be well advised either to take it on to a further generation (something you can only do with a historical) or, better still, to centre it on that peripheral character who grew so strongly in the first that you were threatened that he or she might bid for the limelight.

You probably felt great regret at having to say firmly, 'Down!' to this character, recognising the potential there but wisely keeping it away from centre stage; now is your chance to develop it, building a fresh story with a new idea around a character already familiar and raring to go. In this way you can satisfy the readers you have already won and at the same time make your sequel attractive to a new readership. If you are planning a sequel from the outset, it is as well not to cut off the first book so completely that you leave yourself nowhere to go. As Douglas Adams, author of *The Hitch-hiker's Guide to the Galaxy* (science fiction could be described as the historical of the future) said in an interview, 'Don't blow up the world in chapter one, you may need it later on!'

The way ahead

Publishers and literary agents hold widely varying views on the future of the historical, and it has to be faced that public taste is fickle and easily influenced by the next trend to catch the eye. A few years ago there was an enormous boom in historicals; everyone jumped on the wagon as the rosy prospects glowed, giving us the bodice-ripper, the saga, the blockbuster, the big adventure, the period romance, until the wagon was so overloaded that it crashed, leaving a slump in its wake. The market was for a time flooded with indifferent material which did the genre no good at all. To struggle out of this morass and revive the flagging interest of readers and publishers is no easy task, and one in which only the best can expect to succeed. And here we need to examine the meaning of 'best', which is not merely the most diligent, the most careful, or the most painstaking. It means also the most imaginative and, perhaps above all, the most original.

Into whatever category a book may fall, it must have something to distinguish it, some special quality which in itself defies description. When a British editor was asked at a seminar the time-honoured question, 'What are publishers looking for?', she replied, 'The truth is that we don't know what we're looking for; but when we see it, it shines from the page.' It must surely be just that quality which marks out the winners of the Georgette Heyer award among the hundred and fifty to two hundred entries pouring in each year.

Going full time

At some point after your first work has been published, especially if it has gone well and to some acclaim, your publisher is likely to say, 'Don't give up the day job!' At the time it will feel like a put-down, a polite euphemism for 'You're not really a writer.'

In fact it is not, although it may take a little time to appreciate the wisdom of these words. What you're being told is, in effect, that money from writing is erratic, and comes in large − or unpredictably small − chunks at quite long intervals; if you are faced with the necessity to write to pay the mortgage, the gas bill and everything else, the quality of your work is likely to suffer, if only because you are going to have to pump it out with unceasing regularity to keep your chin above water; this is when you can become a slave to deadlines, dare not pass up an opportunity to write anything that pays, and may be tempted to rush it or to lose concentration through worrying too much.

It may also be that your publisher, being human, would like to feel free to turn down a book that doesn't quite warrant publication without the knowledge that by doing so he is putting you on the breadline, but that is no reason to doubt his sincerity in advising you. The advice is sound, at least for the time being.

When you have established yourself with a readership, have learned how to pace yourself so that you are no longer a prey to hysteria or panic, it will be a different matter. Eventually you may come to a crossroads in your career when you have to give up either your writing or daily job.

If you are a dedicated and obsessive writer this point will surely come: when it does, try not to relinquish the steady salary until you have made enough from your writing *alone* to keep you going until you can expect the next advance. Be realistic in your assessment, remembering that it may be a matter of several years.

Whatever you do, don't give up your job and *then* start to write. I have known very promising writers to fall into this trap, only to retire from the field disappointed and increasingly embittered.

All in all, keep on writing for the love of it for as long as you can. It is the best of all reasons from any point of view.

14
Better Luck
Next Time?

Well, perhaps it didn't all happen quite like that. After all, it doesn't always, and you may be among the disheartened who tell me with sighs, 'I had a lovely letter, but they didn't take the book. They said. . . .' and here follows a paragraph or two of advice which, could the writer only realise it, is a great encouragement and a rare privilege, since most people only get a printed rejection slip, wailing in their turn: 'Why can't they tell you *why* they don't want it!'

The simple answer is that publishers are just too busy to write to you *unless they think you show real promise*. So take heart, you lucky receivers of letters: somebody up there thinks you are on your way.

The great value of these brief comments, cold and unfeeling as they may seem to you in your hyper-sensitive state, is that they show you where your strengths — and weaknesses — lie. So sit down quietly, dry your tears, and take note of what is said.

Most early writings are a mixture of lacklustre passages and intermittent flashes of brilliance, and a publisher's comments can be invaluable in showing you which is which. It may be that you were misdirecting your effort into something which wasn't right for your particular abilities.

'Sound research — not enough warmth for a romance ... ' This suggests that you have tried to write a love story when your real interest lay in quite different aspects of the social history of the period. Possibly you cluttered the emotional storyline with lengthy dissertations on the politics of the time, or gave more space than was warranted to the differences between the heroine's father and her suitor. Examine your priorities, and see if you would do better to try another category.

You may have a clever and devious mind, which, combined with a strong grasp of the period, could produce a brilliant historical mystery, but instead have beaten your brains out on a light romance which isn't really you.

'Good characterisation — confusing plot' If you like to go very deeply into your characters, you could have done better to concentrate on bringing them to life in a fairly simple setting than to submerge them in a highly complicated plot which, though it may be the life's blood of the blockbuster, is more likely to obscure than enhance your particular talent in a book of average length. This kind of skill often goes with a flair for stirring the emotions of the reader, and needs little to enhance it other than a convincing storyline.

If you are a man, you may have been led to believe that you shouldn't try writing 'romance' (in its broadest sense, this being a novel whose core is the relationship between the sexes), but if that is where your instinct draws you it is quite untrue: you have only to think of Tolstoy's *Anna Karenina* or Hardy's *Tess of the D'Urbervilles* to recognise it as a misconception.

' . . . but we liked your style of writing. Don't give up.' This, perhaps the most frustrating of all comments, may usually be taken to mean that you just haven't hit the spot. In other words, you didn't find the right category for you. Perhaps you are a woman, with a wistful longing to write a big adventure, who lets preconceptions ('big adventures are written by men for men'/'only women can write romance' etc . . .) force her into a mould that didn't fit. I know of one writer whose best thing is undoubtedly the vivid and realistic battle scene in one of her books; it seems not to occur to her to tackle the real adventure. Being a woman, she continues to write romance.

If this was your problem, think again; remember the success of Vivien Stewart, who began as a romantic novelist and moved on through a long list of maritime historicals to ever-increasing acclaim.

Undoubtedly it takes a writer with a special gift for communicating excitement to do it successfully, but who is to say that that writer is not you? If this is what you really want, try it. Thoroughly research the weapons of your chosen period, their uses, advantages and drawbacks, learn all you can about shipping and other means of travel; and if you plan to write about piracy on the high seas make sure you know how rough, dirty, uncomfortable and restricted were the conditions of the real pirates (no pale imitations of the dashing but well scrubbed and deodorised Errol Flynn). Then think yourself into the skins of your protagonists and take that leap into the dark. You may turn out to be another Alexandre Dumas — although we'd rather hail you as the one and only Joe/Jane Bloggs.

'The story lacked pace/sagged in the middle/tailed off . . .
Maybe you did tackle an adventure, which ran to blockbuster length and didn't realise how hard it would be to fill every page with movement without one or more sub-plots to help it along.

'Disjointed by confusing sub-plots' Perhaps you did realise that these were needed, but made the story disjointed by dodging back and forth too freely between them without due consideration for the main storyline. Ideally, the protagonists in each plot should interconnect so that the main line is enhanced rather than confused; *Gone With the Wind* sets us a good example in the way the story of Melanie and Ashley Wilkes interweaves with that of Scarlett and Rhett Butler without ever hindering the action or becoming intrusive.

'Not enough steam/throb for this type of fiction'   Perhaps you tried a 'hot historical', with an eye to the financial rewards rather than enthusiasm for your subject. The bodice-ripper is also a kind of adventure, but essentially a sexual one. Here, emphasis is on titillation and arousal, and you need to enjoy this kind of writing to be able to sustain it successfully throughout. If you didn't enjoy it, if you had to force yourself to do it, it probably showed through, with the result that your true potential wasn't fully realised.

In almost all of the above cases, the problem has been that the writer has allowed him or herself to be nudged off course, either by her own preconceptions or the misguided opinions of others: i.e. if you are a certain kind of person you should write a certain kind of book. This is nonsense. The majority of romantic fiction − some pretty steamy − is written by little old ladies whom you would never suspect of even reading it; searing dramas are written by quiet school teachers and horrific murders hatched by patient wives and mothers (perhaps there's a message there?)

The important thing is to find out what *you* as an individual do best, and make the most of it. Never be inhibited about writing what you really want to. For example, you might have wanted to write a nostalgia novel but thought it too risky to attempt because you are too young to have lived through the period. In fact, you might have done better with it than the old timer who thinks he knows it all. It is fatally easy to remember something with great clarity, only to discover that it wasn't exactly where, or when, or how we have recalled it. The very things we think we know are those which turn out to be wrong; a young writer with a clear mind uncluttered by corrupted recollections of the past, has as good a chance, or better, of doing it as well as anyone else. So if that is what you really wanted, but were side-tracked into doing something else that wasn't successful, try it.

To sum up: make the most of those depressing letters of rejection. Assimilate those unpalatable truths, and benefit from them. They could just make the difference between non-achievement and eventual success.

15
Wisdom From
on High

To conclude, we have the benefit of personal advice from successful historical authors and others connected with the genre, to whom I extend grateful thanks for their generosity in making these contributions.

Elizabeth Byrd (*Immortal Queen, Maid of Honour, The Flowers of the Forest*) Despite its authentic background of the London Plague, *Forever Amber* taught me what *not* to do. Amber was involved in a series of such monotonous sex scenes that, in the trade, it was called *Forever Under*. There were no contrasts in the seductions, and therefore no peaks of excitement. When outlining a historical novel I select the most dramatic events and try to create at least four 'peaks' of them. These are the scenes that will persuade a publisher to buy and create memories for the reader.

Winston Graham (The *Poldark* series) I think the most important element in writing a historical novel is that the book should have a historical truth as well as a truth to human nature. Man has not changed, but his reaction to certain life patterns has changed. Unless the writer can understand these and transmit this understanding to the reader, his characters are simply modern people in fancy dress.

But one mustn't become too preoccupied with history. Avoid the smell of midnight oil. Novels are about life. A successful historical novel strikes a delicate balance in which the characters are of their time but are not weighted down by its trappings.

Elizabeth Grey (book reviewer) As a reviewer, reading scores of historical novels a year, I look for something new, fresh, original – an unusual period, a different twist. The Tudors and Victorians are grossly over-written (if I read about another intrepid Victorian girl fighting for independence I'll scream).

And 'ware copies of other, successful, original writers; their work will only show up your carbon copies for what they are. (Poor Georgette Heyer!)

Finally, don't try to jump on a rolling band-wagon. The chances are it will have vanished over the horizon before your book reaches the editor's desk.

Susan Kay (*Legacy*)   I find efficient organisation of research one of the most vexing aspects of historical writing. I seem to be permanently swamped by an unwieldy mass of information, while the little details I really need to know constantly elude me. During the years it took to complete *Legacy* there were many occasions when I almost consigned the whole manuscript to the dustbin.

However bad an early draft may seem, it is quite likely to contain certain basic facts, ideas or phrases that could be utilised at a later stage. Unless you are quite certain that your interest in a subject has terminated, don't be tempted to destroy what you have already written out of frustration.

Michael Legat (publisher for 35 years, author of *Mario's Vineyard*)   Among other historical research, check carefully on the clothes your characters wear – both on top and underneath! I am sure that what we wear affects our behaviour. And make sure that the names you use are in period and different enough from each other not to confuse the reader.

John McLaughlin (literary agent)   My personal (and, mostly, professional) taste is for those historical novels which place in equal focus the differences and the similarities between 'then' and 'now'. I lose interest most rapidly when offered either modern characters in fancy dress, or layers of period detail and dialogue which obscure story and character alike.

Diane Pearson (*Czardas, The Summer of the Barshinskeys*; also a senior editor at Corgi and a resident judge of the Georgette Heyer Award)   In my view historicals fall into two distinct categories. The first is the period novel which covers the final years of the last century and most of the twentieth – roughly, the 1880s to the Second World War. This category is, in my opinion, far easier to write. There are the family memories recounted by old people, passed on sometimes at first hand, and plenty of old letters, records, newspapers to cannibalise, and soak up period. The true historical, the other category, the 'before living memory' period is much harder to bring alive. And one *must* bring it alive, otherwise the book is doomed. Characters, be they early Roman or Elizabethan, must be so real that the reader instantly identifies with them. In other words, the writer has to *become* Anne Boleyn, to feel as she felt, to be capricious, afraid, ambitious, or whatever other qualities you care to attribute to her.

The commonest trap into which the hopeful novelist falls is that of speech style. Phrases like 'in the Year of Our Lord 1436' (or even worse, 'the year of our Lord 1926' – everyone knows people didn't think like that in 1926) instantly label the book as a contrived piece. You should find some subtler and more realistic way of letting your reader know the period of your book. Stilted dialogue, an attempt to write in the colloquialism of the time, always makes for a heavy and unappetising book. Equally disastrous is turning the dialogue into recognisable everyday modern speech i.e. 'She was four months gone when she married Henry VIII.' The books that ring true (see Norah Lofts and Ellis Peters) are those written in just good, basic English, no frills, no slang, no contrived historical clichés.

So, to sum up – point one: *become your central characters*, breathe life into them, make them real however ancient they are. Point two: don't attempt any writing style except that of good, straight, non-colloquial basic English.

Jean Plaidy (*Murder Most Royal, A Health Unto His Majesty* and many others)   Historical novels are for those people who like to learn a little history and polish up what they already know, but, most importantly, like to be entertained while they are doing it.

This is a *novel* not merely a collection of facts. It is a great mistake to overload the book with details. They may be fascinating to the writer but less so to the reader; and after all if readers want details they can look these up. This does not mean that there should be inaccuracies to suit the story. One should avoid this at all costs for it creates confusion and lack of trust. Moreover reality is often stranger than fiction and it has the added lustre of being true.

It is most important to bring to life those characters who have hitherto been only names in the reader's mind. The reader must see them as real people, to love them or hate them and care what happens to them. Tragedy, comedy, drama should all be highlighted. Dialogue must sound natural to the characters and the period. This is not difficult because fortunately there seemed to be quite a number of people who liked to peer through keyholes or hide behind the arras, listen to what was said and done, and then dash off to scribble it down. When the reader is unable to tell the difference between your dialogue and this written by eyewitnesses you will know you have succeeded.

The great motive is to show those people who previously thought history a bit of a bore that it is one of the most fascinating subjects on earth.

Rona Randall (*Dragonmede, The Mating Dance*)   Before I can write about a period a sense of *belonging* to it is vital. I can then think and feel and talk as if it were my own. Otherwise it would be written by an outsider: detached, unreal, unconvincing. With *The Mating*

Dance, a theatrical novel, I inevitably chose the late Victorian age because, in my teens, I had toured with old pros and been fascinated by their reminiscences, absorbing their views and their jargon like blotting paper. I have also been steeped in the Edwardian era, thanks to my mother's stories of her girlhood.

But other associations can bring a period alive. Active participation in ceramics sparked *The Drayton Legacy* and its sequel, *The Potter's Niece*, so the growth of the Potteries in the 18th century was again a natural choice and research was enjoyable. And that is another essential — *enjoy* the period you are writing about, and your readers will enjoy it too. If you don't, they won't.

Jasper Ridley, historical biographer (*Henry VIII, Elizabeth I*)   If — and this is a very important 'if' — the historical novelist has a thorough understanding of the period about which he is writing, he may often get nearer to the truth than the historian or historical biographer. Most of the things which men and women, even famous men and women, did in their lives were not recorded by contemporary letter-writers, diarists or chroniclers, and so the historian and bio-grapher cannot mention them; the novelist can, and may sense, by intuition, what really happened.

Provided he resists the temptation to turn his historical characters into 20th-century people, the historical novelist can really bring the past to life.

Rosemary Sutcliff (*The Eagle of the Ninth, The Rider of the White Horse*, etc.)   Never make the mistake of thinking that you must use *all* the fruits of your research. You may not need more than a tenth of it; but the other nine-tenths will not be wasted, because it will have enriched and filled out your own knowledge of the place/period/ subject of your story.

Nothing is worse for a book than to be clotted with too much and too obvious knowledge, which will stick out like the lumps in a badly made porridge.

Anne Worboys (*A Kingdom for the Bold*)   When writing a historical novel, in order to convey the full flavour of the time, I find it most helpful, before starting work in the morning, to immerse myself in a few pages of Jane Austen or Dickens. To a lesser extent, The Brontës. Don't worry about plagiarism. The particular genius of these writers defies imitation. Nonetheless, try to absorb rather than read. Even a glance at the spine of the book on the shelf can effect a kind of discipline.

Again, after stopping in the evening, read a page or two of the same. Hopefully, one will then see whether the day's work is or is not up to standard. Dispiriting, of course, if one discovers at that hour the tone is wrong, but the chances are anger at oneself will fire the subconscious overnight.

Barbara Willard (*The Queen of the Pharisees' Children, The Iron Lily*) Historical fiction is about *us — then*. Social historians offer amazing insights into the everyday past; it is not difficult to insinuate ourselves into a given period. We were not always the sons or daughters of the manor; I often remind myself that I could have been born the thirteenth child of the cowherd's exhausted wife. I come indoors from milking in the dark winter dawn; I am cold, wet and hungry — and there is not wood enough to mend the fire. Any such image cuts out captains and kings, tapestries and banquets, and offers a perfect starting point.

(Barbara Willard won the Whitbread Literary Award for *The Queen of the Pharisees' Children*, and the Guardian Award for Children's Literature for *The Iron Lily*.)

Alexandra Jones (*off to a flying start with her first novel Mandalay*) Start *today*! Time is always there, use it. There is no tomorrow when it comes to writing and getting your work accepted. Temptation is all around: temptation to avoid in any way possible facing that blank sheet of paper — shopping, visiting, chatting with friends, going to the pictures, watching *Dallas*, coffee mornings, I'll just pull out that sunchair for minutes — endless temptation. Avoid it by repeating in front of the typewriter/word processor/exercise book 'Lead us not into temptation!'

Never, never give up!

You will have noticed that all these writers, representing as they do every degree of success from the top of the ladder to the first rung, are in agreement on some salient points; nevertheless, each has a different priority, his or her own special approach to the subject, some of which may be seen to be at variance with others. This is perfectly natural. There are as many ways of writing as there are writers.

The one thing they all have in common is that they have found the golden needle. May you find yours.

Enjoy your writing, and may good luck attend you. Don't confuse achievement with success. Even if you never make a penny from your writing, you will still have the incomparable satisfaction of having created a world that no-one else could have made, and peopled it with the children of your own imagination.

Savour that knowledge: revel in it. That is the reality of achievement. The only true failure is in not having tried.

Index